DYSPRAXIA 5–11

A PRACTICAL GUIDE

CHRISTINE MACINTYRE

David Fulton Publishers Ltd
Ormond House, 26–27 Boswell Street, London WC1N 3JZ

www.fultonpublishers.co.uk

First published in Great Britain by David Fulton Publishers 2001

British Library Cataloguing in Publication Data
A catalogue record for this book is available from the British Library

ISBN 1–85346–784–7

Typeset by Textype Typesetters, Cambridge
Printed in Great Britain by The Cromwell Press Ltd, Wilts.

Contents

Foreword

This is an unusual book for many reasons. It gives clear explanations about dyspraxia which, until recently, has been a difficult co-ordination disorder for non-specialists to learn about. It gives practical advice to parents and teachers whose children must cope with the limitations imposed on them by dyspraxia. It gives research which shows that, with the right encouragement, children with dyspraxia can themselves see the reasons for the difficulties they face, and they can flourish.

This is a genuinely educational book. Its purpose is not simply that, as readers, we come to learn about children in the age range 5 to 11 who have dyspraxia, but also that we understand enough, and feel enough, to respond to them properly, helpfully and positively.

This is Dr. Christine Macintyre's second book about dyspraxia. She is the kind of person who wants her work to make difference for the good. Having read her book, I am confident that it does.

Margot Cameron-Jones
Professor of Teacher Education
University of Edinburgh

Acknowledgements

This is Hannah. She has dyspraxia. The book explains Hannah's difficulties and shows how despite them, she remains a loving and lovely child. The book is written to help those who have children, who care for children, who teach children or who are children like Hannah, for she is not alone. The numbers of children with dyspraxia are increasing – or perhaps our awareness of the syndrome has caused us to identify more. Whatever the reason, it is imperative that all these children, and that means around 8–10 per cent of youngsters, are given specific help so that they may overcome their problems in the best way they can. Dyspraxic children may have a label – but that label need not endure, for although at this moment there is no cure, help and practice can make a huge difference.

Many children like Hannah have contributed to the compilation of this book. My thanks go to them and to their parents and teachers for allowing me to share in developing work which has been shown to help. Suddenly these children are realising that they are as important as any other children. They are gaining confidence and achieving more. When we have given them belief in themselves, and when we hear them say, 'Yes we can do it too', our job will be done.

Introduction

As children move from home, nursery or play group into the primary school, they face a significant number of new challenges and these increase in number and complexity as the years pass. Increasingly, children must take responsibility for thinking ahead to organise their day, learning and practising new skills, completing pieces of work, looking out for each other and making friends. This is not an untroubled path for any child, but those with specific difficulties need extra understanding and support if they are to reach their full potential.

Children with dyspraxia come into this category. These children have a coordination disorder which makes coping at home and at school both taxing and tiring. Without help they are sure to underachieve. Those who are there to offer the support they need must understand the complexities of dyspraxia, realise that it impinges upon all aspects of coping and learning, appreciate that progress will be erratic, no matter how hard the children try and, above all, help them to stay positive despite the frustrations that 'not being able to do' brings. This is the important message for everyone concerned. Stay positive. Recognise that 'these children can be helped' (Caan 1998). Children with dyspraxia are likely to be of average or above average intelligence. Their intellectual ability means that they can understand what is wrong, learn to keep their difficulties in perspective and understand how interventions are structured to help them; increasingly so as they mature. They also look just the same as other children. While this is a good thing, sometimes they are denied the understanding that a more obvious disability would bring. 'If I had a broken leg, people would know and make allowances, said Craig, adding, 'but no one even knows what dyspraxia is!'

And so this book sets out to explain dyspraxia and how the condition impacts on children of primary school age. Based on a developmental framework, it covers the myriad of influences affecting and affected by dyspraxia and emphasises how each child must be carefully observed and accurately assessed. This is to ensure that intervention can build on the children's strengths as well as help them overcome their difficulties, as far as they can. It also shows how a supportive environment with the correct resources, both human and physical, can do much to relieve the pressures children experience. It offers strategies to help. I hope that they do.

CHAPTER 1

Explaining dyspraxia

The Dyspraxia Foundation (Dyspraxia Trust 1997) describes the condition as,

> An impairment or immaturity in the organisation of movement which leads to associated problems with language, perception and thought.

This is a useful description but as it encompasses the whole condition, it is quite complex, and those who are interested in finding out about dyspraxia for the first time usually have a number of more basic questions. These need to be considered separately before the key issues are brought together again to show how apt the quotation is. If parents and teachers, and indeed everyone who is in close contact with the children, do not fully understand the condition and take the most appropriate steps to help, it is possible, even likely that all aspects of the children's development will suffer. This book has been written to provide that understanding and to show how the right kind of help can reduce the negative effects of having dyspraxia.

What do people want to know? The most usual questions are:

- What is dyspraxia?
- What difficulties do the children have?
- Why should this be?
- How many children are affected?
- What can be done to help?

Let's begin with the first question.

What is dyspraxia?

There are many signs and symptoms which indicate that a child could have dyspraxia and these will be discussed briefly in this introductory chapter and in more detail in the ones which concern each aspect of development. The aim of the book is to give parents and teachers a comprehensive account of the condition. It must be stressed from the start, however, that it is not likely that any one child will have all of the symptoms! Children have different blends of difficulties at different levels of severity. This can make accurate diagnosis quite tricky, especially as the children's 'performance', i.e. the level of success they have in tackling movement tasks, can vary depending on the setting – and on how the children are able to respond at that particular time. The things the children can do quite well can fluctuate from day to day. Teachers often say, 'But if he could do it yesterday – why not today?' Perhaps the child is too tired or perhaps, due to his short term memory deficit, he has forgotten the way he did it before. This is why it is important to make and record observations at different times of the day and in different situations. The fact that individual children have their own pattern of 'signs and symptoms' also means that one recipe for intervention will not do, for although motor programmes can be generally helpful, planning for specific, individual difficulties must also be carried through.

One 'positive' which is a comfort to parents and which should be remembered by everyone coming into contact with the children, is that they are likely to be of average or above average intelligence. Dyspraxia is not a general pervasive disorder; these children do not have global developmental delay, i.e. a general low level of attainment. This means that affected children can understand what is wrong, how intervention works for them and how they need to persevere and practise, increasingly so as they mature. Children with dyspraxia also look just the same as other children and while this can sometimes deny them the sympathy that a more obvious disability would bring, no one would want them to have to overcome 'looking different' as well. Kirby (1999a) explains that these children have a 'hidden handicap'. This means that other people have to be able to recognise what is causing the difficulties and be prepared to learn how to help. Nor do they have a clear neurological disorder such as cerebral palsy or an illness which causes physical pain or gets worse. And so, although dyspraxia brings a number of problems and many frustrations, there are plus points, and appreciating these and remembering them when things get tough as well as building on the success which practice can bring, is the way to keep morale and self-esteem high.

The name itself provides a brief description of the condition, for 'dys' means 'faulty' and 'praxis' means 'the ability to use the body as a skilled tool', and indeed it is usually a movement coordination difficulty of some kind which indicates that all is not well. Children with dyspraxia find moving easily (i.e. with efficient, flowing movements) difficult, especially when new challenges have to be faced. These children do learn to walk and run, write and talk but they often develop these skills – their motor milestones – later than others do, just within the 'normal' time span, and they never reach the same level of performance. Practised movements do improve, and this is good news which should give lots of encouragement to children with dyspraxia, for it shows that intervention can be successful, but nonetheless they do have a fundamental problem with coordination which needs to be addressed early to maximise the chance of improvement. Sadly, at present there is no cure, although ongoing research, e.g. into the metabolism of fatty acids and in using coloured lenses or overlays as some children with dyslexia do, is holding out hope that quicker and more successful ways to help will soon be found.

What difficulties do children have?

Coordination is a term that covers different kinds of actions. It depends on the interplay of different movement abilities such as perception, i.e. taking cues from the environment to guide spatial judgments; a good sense of both static and dynamic or moving balance and rhythmic awareness (more detail in Chapter 3). Moreover, there are different kinds of coordination depending on the intrinsic nature of the activity that is to be done.

First, there is whole body coordination which involves the large muscle groups and affects gross motor skills like running, jumping and climbing. Some children have great difficulty in doing these basic movement patterns. One cause is poor muscle tone. If this is the case, and occurs in the pelvic region, running can be affected by lax hip and leg muscles which allow toes to turn in and brush against the legs causing stumbling. To run well, these children need to concentrate hard on controlling their feet to avoid falling, while other children race ahead without giving control a thought. Shoulder laxity prevents control of the arms and so any pulling action where strength is required is very difficult, for example, pulling along a bench takes much time and a great deal of body 'hitching along' to compensate.

It follows that when apparatus needs to be controlled, as in kicking or catching a ball or in batting skills, their difficulties are significantly increased, for these skills call on hand–eye or foot–eye coordination in addition to whole body coordination and this can be overwhelming! Controlling apparatus needs a clear sense of body boundary, i.e. where the body ends and the apparatus begins, as well as visual and spatial awareness to track the flight of the oncoming ball or to judge where to send it. Did you ever think that moving could be so complicated?

Then there is fine motor control which requires the smaller groups of muscles to work in harmony. If they don't, children will have difficulty writing, drawing, sewing and carrying out movements where precision is required. Having said that, children who find writing difficult because they can't find an effective pencil grip or because handwriting involves crossing the midline of the body, often manage keyboard skills with ease. In this activity there is no pencil to control for each hand works largely on its own side of the body. The child can sit upright and be well supported, back held by the chair, feet planted firmly on the floor and the height of the computer can be adjusted to suit. Given these preparations, the children are freed to concentrate at the task in hand. This 'solution' to handwriting problems brings out another positive – there is often a way to circumvent difficulties, and later in the book lots of suggestions are made in the hope that teachers will find them practical and realistic when they have numerous other children to cope with as well.

Children with dyspraxia often hate having to be involved in sporting activities. It is hugely upsetting for children always to be the last to be chosen because they can't play well or can't follow the rules of the game. Having said that, some love to play. This can depend as much on the attitude of the other children as on the temperament of the child himself. Jamie explains, 'I'm not in the best team but a jolly good one. Sometimes I get a bit mixed up when we change ends but everyone just shouts, "Come on Jamie, this way!" Once or twice I've scored an own goal and everyone groaned, but when they saw I was upset the teacher reminded us all that it's only a game and what was the important thing to remember? That everyone should have fun.' So the school ethos can make a huge difference.

Not many dyspraxic children can sustain his happy-go-lucky approach, however, and with the others in mind, the question must be, 'do they have to play?' Could they not have an important 'other' job such as being the scorer? Maybe the children could have a choice of activities, so that they can choose something they enjoy – perhaps downloading information for the class theme from the Internet? Other kinds of activities can sometimes be substituted for those that are too difficult and so make a positive input to the children's day. The best thing is for small groups of children with the same interests to work together in a purposeful and enjoyable way. Then the dyspraxic children can play a full part. Nowadays, classroom assistants could supervise these 'other activities' while the teacher is in the gym or out of doors. It would be wonderful if the stress which dyspraxic children feel acutely, could be relieved in this way.

Middle childhood years

In the junior and middle schools however, children usually have to join in a great range of activities, and this is why age 7–15 is the most difficult time for children with dyspraxia; after that there is more choice and the children can choose activities to suit their strengths. This may be offset by the fact that the developmental path is relatively smooth between age seven and the onset of puberty. A set of important changes happen, but over time. Children begin to form a global self-concept at eight or so but this is still developing at eleven. Gender segregation of friends is complete. There is no sudden rush of hormones or growth spurt at this juncture. Perhaps teachers will worry that if children avoid activities like team games, the others will see them as being 'different' thus increasing their social isolation, or that the children will miss out on 'the very kind of activity they need'. But, from the child's point of view, team games usually mean public humiliation and their potential level of participation is further lowered by the stress this brings. When that happens, this kind of activity is not helpful; these children need a small group perceptual-motor programme specifically designed to help their difficulties (see Chapter 8).

One specific kind of coordination requires the muscles in the lips, mouth and soft palate to work together to produce coherent speech. Children who can't articulate clearly have difficulty in making themselves understood and so they lose confidence in interacting and building relationships and prefer to work and play alone. Sometimes they have difficulty in regulating the tone or pitch of their speech and this can make them reluctant to communicate. This is verbal dyspraxia and for the children who attempt to talk before moving around, it can be the first indication that something is wrong. This is a very different problem to that faced by children who don't understand language and who therefore do not give the correct answers. Children with dyspraxia do understand, but they have difficulty controlling the 'technical equipment' so that it makes the correct response. This links back to the intellectual differences mentioned earlier. Slack muscles in the mouth can also cause dribbling which is socially frowned on. When children with this difficulty lean over their jotter to write, as one example, dribbling onto the page spoils their work and of course this is most upsetting for them. When they have to concentrate so hard on their writing skills, other areas of control tend to give. Having an inclined desk can reduce this problem because then the children don't have to lean so far over their work.

Two-handed coordination is often difficult for children with dyspraxia, especially if the movement task requires them to cross the midline of the body or take their hands behind their back. Tasks like opening a carton of juice or using knives and forks cause difficulty as do visits to the toilet – for this involves undoing buttons or zips, sitting comfortably balanced on the loo, then wiping before getting dressed again – a whole set of complex tasks, made much worse if they have to be done quickly at a certain time of day with another child waiting to go.

Crossing the midline presents huge obstacles for children with dyspraxia. All sorts of daily tasks are affected, e.g. pulling on socks, reaching over to open a door, buttering a roll on a plate! It is as if a wall divides the two halves of their body. Often these children also lack a sense of having a dominant hand and if they are asked to draw a rainbow they will use one hand for the first section of the arc then transfer the pencil to the other hand to complete the pattern. Tying laces can be a nightmare. Unfortunately, children can regard this as a landmark of achievement in the primary school and dyspraxic children get left behind: 'He can't tie his laces yet' – another public declaration which is humiliating and hurtful. Many mums have had cause to bless velcro for all sorts of fastenings and again this is an example of identifying the problem and then searching for ways to overcome it. Some schools, however, won't allow velcro fastenings for shoes and trousers and refuse to have elastic for school ties – and of course no child likes to be different. I wonder if these schools have understood dyspraxia at all? Would they listen if parents tried to explain?

Some children may only experience problems with movements which involve the large muscle groups. While their gross movements, e.g. running and jumping, are clumsy and awkward, they can manage fine movements quite well. Others only experience difficulty when fine motor skills are required; they do not have the dexterity to fasten buttons or do up zips. Not all children have articulation problems. Careful observation and recording of children coping or not coping in different situations is essential if intervention and help is to be targeted successfully. This continuous assessment and recording of encountered difficulties in different situations is essential before specialist help is requested. And of course the benefits and possible disadvantages of giving a child a 'label' and extra programmes of therapy, have to be understood too (see Chapter 2).

Despite their difficulties, children can be helped to improve discrete skills, and this means that when the children are required to do these movements – given time and encouragement and sustained practice – they will be able to cope. However, when the children have to do these or similar actions again in different environments, they have to tackle them as a first time effort. This is because dyspraxic children seem to have no transfer of learning from one situation to another; they do not have the movement recall which allows them to select aspects of the movements they already can do and apply them in a new situation. This means that movements do not become automatic; the planning for each one has to begin anew. When Ayres (1972) defined dyspraxia as 'The inability to plan and execute non-habitual movements', this is what she meant. As a result of this constant concentration – remember how difficult learning to drive was? – the children become tired and dispirited and when on occasions it all becomes too much, screamingly frustrated with all the effort 'just managing' entails. The frustration is made worse when they see other children coping with little effort and lots of success. For dyspraxic children, the day is full of first time challenges and so 'they have a very tiring day' (Chesson *et al.* 1990). For these reasons, those who understand dyspraxia will not urge these children to 'try harder' or to 'do it again, neatly this time', for they are likely to be trying just as hard as they can.

These coordination difficulties belong to the movement execution or 'doing' aspect of dyspraxia and they have been highlighted first because movements which are clumsy and awkward are the most obvious signs that something is amiss. There are two other facets, however, which may well hamper efficient movement. These are the planning and organisation of movement, i.e. the underlying intellectual processes which must be considered in any analysis of dysfunction or impaired action.

Movement then, has three sub-components (Figure 1.1).

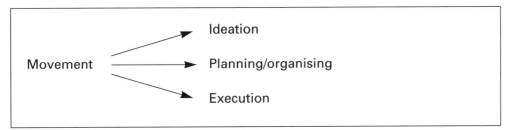

Figure 1.1 The three sub-components of movement

Ideation – knowing what to do

Children who have difficulty with this aspect of movement preparation can often be seen wandering around looking lost, or doing something aimlessly. Usually they stay on the periphery of any activity. This is because they are so unsure of what to do. They may try to copy other children, which can help up to a point, as long as their 'model' is successful in following instructions and as long as the copying causes no resentment. Copying does mean delay however, and if the dyspraxic child is already quite slow at responding to instructions, scolding may follow.

Planning

Children who are poor planners can know what they want to achieve, but have difficulty knowing how to bring their ideas to fruition. Planning involves building a mental model of the action: 'I'll have to jump over that puddle if my shoes are to stay dry', or 'If he hits the ball over there, I'll have to move out to the side to hit it back', or 'If I am going to construct this bridge, I have to find the span then decide on the number of supports . . .'

Organising

Children who are poor organisers have problems ordering the sequence of actions, in deciding what resources they will need, what action should come first, how long each part takes, how much strength each action requires, or where they should go. Getting dressed, that is putting clothes on in the correct order, is really problematic for some children – this is different from not being able to do the intrinsic actions, e.g. fastening buttons. Sometimes children manage the first part of a sequence of actions or follow the first instruction, but then, due to poor short term memory, they forget what comes next and either stop, bewildered, or 'do their own thing', which again is rarely appreciated!

If any of these difficulties are present, then it is not difficult to see that the children will need more time to sort themselves out. So often they are urged to 'hurry up', just to keep up with the others or to arrive somewhere in time. 'What is *valuable* time?' asked four-year-old Peter. Obviously he had been found guilty of wasting it. Having to hurry however, acts against movement being coordinated and so it is clumsy: the child misses the ball or collapses onto a chair, knocks it over and both clatter to the floor, or he misjudges the space between himself and objects and bumps into whatever or whoever is in his path. One fairly exasperated teacher wrote, 'You'll know this child, he is forever standing on your feet' – a picture which evokes a wry chuckle.

Executing

This concerns actually carrying out the movement with all the movement ability requirements such as strength and balance and control coming into play. Alongside that, the perceptual judgments which inform the action must be accurate (see also Chapter 3).

Analysing planning, organising and carrying out movement

It goes without saying that when children have difficulties, movement analysis to find the exact reason must precede intervention. Correcting the movement pattern is only going to be of minimal use if, for example, the underlying strength is lacking. This is complex but essential if help is to be targeted correctly.

For those of us who do not have these difficulties, it could be salutary to take a moment to think of the planning and organising which children must cope with before they enter the classroom at all and before they have the support of any teacher.

Jack

Example 1

Picture Jack, aged nine, coming into school on a wet day. The normal routine of waiting outside has been disrupted by bad weather and the cloakroom is noisy with children bustling around divesting themselves of a multitude of anoraks and wellies. Jack must find his own peg, but today it has disappeared beneath a pile of coats. He doesn't want to ask for help or he might be teased and the noise is confusing him even further.

Then, he must get out of his wellies and put on his trainers. While he tries to do this, his boots get kicked out of the way. Really agitated now, he chases them in his socks which get soaked and so won't slip into his trainers. The struggle to get them on means that he has to balance on one foot and cross his hands over the midline of his body. This is impossibly difficult and he has to give up.

After that, lunch boxes have to be placed in the correct place – where's that again? – and notes from Mum have to be retrieved from his schoolbag and taken to the classroom. This means he must undo his schoolbag and because he clutches the bag tightly to his chest, all his books spill out onto the wet floor. Jack knows this will be discovered and he cries and so desperately wants to go home. The other children laugh and his books join the kicking game.

When Jack does get to the classroom, he discovers he hasn't left his coat in the cloakroom and he is sent back. By this time he is so unhappy that he is not sure whether the cloakroom is round that corner or the next one. He sits down for a rest and watches the infant children coming in, loses track of time and when the teacher sends someone to find him, he knows he will be scolded again – even though he's not sure why. Poor Jack! What a start to the day and it's not nine o'clock yet!

This mini scenario shows some of the more subtle implications of not being able to move well – it demonstrates the 'waves' which spread out to embarrass and confuse the child and negatively affect his self-esteem. Few seven-year-old children have the level of altruism or courage to stand up for a dyspraxic child, especially as that child, used to being mocked, may react inappropriately, not realising that a friend has come to help. The scenario also shows why 'the primary objective of all methods of intervention must be to improve the child's ability to function in everyday life' (Sugden and Henderson 1994).

This means that parents can play a huge part in helping, firstly through understanding the condition, then using routine tasks and everyday coping skills as practices. Realising this can demystify the 'treatment' and make it much more manageable for many parents. Specific therapies can be required for children with specific difficulties but many have no access or do not wish this kind of intervention. Kirby (1999a) explains that when children are tired, parents are anxious and siblings are jealous of the time given to one child, therapy-at-home time can become fraught, with tears and ragings and eventually it may be abandoned. Then everyone feels guilty and any hope of progress seems remote.

And of course, all children can be clumsy and forgetful and disorganised at times. The Dyspraxia Foundation urges us not to call every child who displays some of these characteristics some of the time, dyspraxic. Dyspraxia is an enduring condition and although some days are better than others, dyspraxic children have a consistently low level of motor performance. The American Psychiatric Association (1994) sets out five criteria for the condition they call developmental coordination disorder. They are:

1. There is a marked impairment in the development of motor coordination.
2. The impairment significantly interferes with academic achievement or activities of daily living.
3. The coordination difficulties are not due to a general medical condition, e.g. cerebral palsy, hemiplegia or muscular dystrophy.

4. It is not a pervasive developmental disorder.
5. If a developmental delay is evident, the motor difficulties are in excess of those usually associated with it.

These can usefully guide any diagnosis of dyspraxia, or in their terms 'developmental coordination disorder'.

Why should this be?

Children with dyspraxia have difficulty in interpreting perceptual information, i.e. clues which come from the environment through the senses to be organised in the brain and then relayed to the muscles to produce efficient and effective movement. (Figure 1.2)

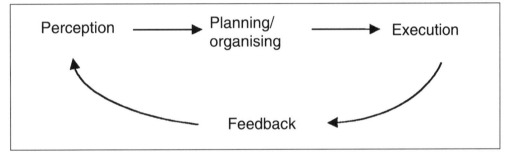

Figure 1.2 Perception: An input/output model

If the child's perceptual system, i.e. all the sensory information coming to the brain, is incorrect in some way, then the sequence of events which follow will be faulty too. If, for example, a child sees the table as being nearer than it really is, then the cup of juice which is to go on it crashes to the floor, whereas if he sees it as being further away, then he will be onto it before he can stop and bumping and clattering result. The child has not been careless, he has followed the spatial information he has received. This explains why everyday actions which happen in the same settings and therefore can be called routine, practised actions are much more efficient than new movements carried out in unfamiliar places. Habitual or practised movements provide feedback each time they occur and so the children gradually manage to make adjustments until the action is correct. This, of course, can't apply when movements are being tried for the first time and so these are clumsy, often causing irritation, even retaliation when bumping into others happens, or when spills down clothes or onto carpets occur!

A last difficulty which must be considered, is that some children retain some of the primitive reflexes which should have been inhibited through maturation. This means that if the sensitive areas on their bodies are stimulated, perhaps by a T-shirt rubbing, then movement which is quite involuntary occurs – as much to the child's surprise as anyone else's. These movements, which are not under the conscious control of the child, may take the form of fidgeting or twitching or shoulder shrugging depending on the region that is activated. They can be very distracting to the teacher who has just settled her class and can as such be a source of negative input for the dyspraxic child.

How many children are affected?

- Eight to ten per cent of children have some degree of dyspraxia.
- Two per cent of these children will be severely affected.
- Boys:girls are affected 4:1 but when girls have the condition, they tend to be more severely affected.
- There is often overlap with another syndrome, e.g. 50 per cent of children with dyspraxia will also be dyslexic. It is very difficult to find the 'pure' child dyspraxic.

(Kirby 1999b)

What does this mean? Well, for parents, these figures can offer some comfort in that they are not alone in having a child with movement difficulties. But they can be also be frightening or daunting if they show that another disorder could be making the diagnosis worse. Thinking positively however, this does mean that there can be more than one source of support and help (see Appendix 5). At this moment in time, more dyslexia than dyspraxia groups are established and so are further on in being able to offer support and advice. These could be a useful first line of enquiry. There is also more information in books now (see the Bibliography) and currently dyspraxia is getting more research support. The Dyspraxia Foundation (see Bibliography) is a major source of support.

Teachers will possibly find these figures startling because they mean that there are likely to be two, even three children with some degree of dyspraxia in every class. Many will deny this until they understand the condition and develop the eyes to let them see. In fact one teacher told me, 'Now that I know what to look for, they've all got it!' Many early years' teachers have told me that they 'know there is something wrong', but they are not sure what is causing the difficulty and so they are reluctant to suggest to parents that their child has a problem. This is because the parents are likely to be upset by any suggestion that their child is not coping well and if the difficulty is caused by developmental delay, rather than dyspraxia, maturation, hand in hand with appropriate teaching, may well sort it out. The teachers, however, have to recognise the possibility that dyspraxia could be the diagnosis and take steps to intervene and help – after all fun activities for the whole nursery, e.g. songs like 'hands, shoulders, knees and toes', can be enjoyed by all the children, even though they have been specially chosen to help the youngsters who have poor body awareness and are not too sure where their knees and toes are. (Lots of suggestions to help this age group are in Chapter 8, and *Dyspraxia in the Early Years*, also published by David Fulton Publishers, is specifically written for this age group.)

But when the difficulties persist beyond nursery, time is no longer on their side. Children as young as six see themselves as incompetent. If they move clumsily or drop things, they arouse conflict and anger in adults. They know they have displeased but are not sure why, and so they think, 'I'm no use'. And once they begin to evaluate themselves in this negative way, they generalise this assessment to other aspects of coping and learning. They don't say, 'I'm a bit clumsy at writing', or 'I'm not good at football', but 'I'm no use at all'. They begin to believe they can't do anything well. And so teachers have a huge responsibility both in helping the children and in informing the parents who will decide if they wish to have their child tested with recognised tests, possibly the ABC tests (the Movement Assessment Battery for Children), and, depending on the results, possibly request physiotherapy or occupational therapy to help. There are also many classroom opportunities and strategies that can help these children – these are set out alongside the difficulties described in each chapter and in Chapter 7. By age five or six intervention is vital. It can be built into the classroom routine. No other child will be harmed by taking part. The sooner the intervention happens, the more effective it is likely to be. All children have a right to an education which will allow them to fulfil their potential. Everyone must ensure that children with dyspraxia have this too.

The following chapters will go into much more detail and show the implications of dyspraxia for the children in each aspect of their development. They will give suggestions and strategies which have helped other children. At this moment in time, dyspraxia is claiming more attention from those who have the resources to help. We need to be sure that they are targeted in the right direction, i.e. to help the children themselves.

A summary of signs and symptoms

- Difficulty in producing coordinated, fluent action;
- poor sense of balance;
- difficulty in knowing what to do and judging what kind of response is acceptable;

- difficulty in retaining more than one piece of information, e.g. story sequences or any 'do this and then that' kind of organisation;
- weak muscle tone impacting on the execution of movement patterns;
- poor body awareness, i.e. knowing where the body parts are in relation to one another;
- poor kinesthetic awareness, i.e. knowing where the body is in space, which affects spatial judgments – how far and in what direction;
- ipse lateral hand use, i.e. using the hand on its own side of the body;
- lack of clear bilateral dominance, i.e. no clear picture of a stronger side. Mixed dominance leads to directional confusion, i.e. reversal of letters, numbers and words and also difficulty in asymmetrical movements such as tying laces or using cutlery or holding a paper in one hand while cutting out with the other.

The difficulties appear never-ending and some unfortunate youngsters have lots. However, other children may only have difficulty in a few areas. All the children need lots of positive reinforcement when things go well and sympathy, understanding and tolerance on a bad day.

What can be done to help?

Once parents and teachers understand the range of difficulties their children have, they will be anxious to remove all the obstacles they can from their home and school day. There are different ways to help, depending on the age of the children – newly-into-school children will need pictures and colour coding while older ones will be able to follow directional arrows or written instructions. These aids are time consuming to make at the outset, but this is time well spent as they do help the children to be independent. The children themselves can choose the pictures, decide on their favourite colour for colour coding and generally help prepare the resources, so learning about them at the same time.

The children's difficulties will be in:

- knowing what to do;
- getting organised; and
- getting it done.

And of course input must be helpful to the specific difficulties each child has. Parents and teachers need to anticipate what their children need to be able to do to 'get there' with as little stress as possible for everyone in the family. What is the best way to do this? (See also Chapters 6 and 7.)

- Think of each part of the day separately and decentre, i.e. visualise the kind of hurdles children are likely to face.
- Identify the child's difficulties and prepare a checklist of 'things to be done' (see Figure 1.3).
- Use colour coding whenever possible – red dots at home and at school help the children identify their own toothbrush, blazer, PE kit, wellingtons, jotter etc. and this saves both time and squabbles. A supportive teacher could have the child in the red group so that colour coding was not so obvious, or other groups might use different colours to help identify their work too.
- Use numbering to help the children follow the order of things to be done. The children could paint the numbers and Blu-Tack them, e.g. on their bedroom wall, so that clothes could be set out in the correct order, thus simplifying getting dressed.
- Have a free standing kitchen timer to help the children realise how long passages of time last – for some find it difficult to understand the concept of ten minutes or half an hour. The sand running out gives a visual warning and this helps them be ready in time, saving last minute hassles!

Not all children have the same number or severity of difficulties, so not all of these strategies will be needed – it also may be possible to discard some quite quickly and this can give a real sense of progression. The checklists make sure all the difficulties are recognised, perhaps by brothers or sisters who can become impatient, and so they are first line attempts to see what can be done:

a) to develop the child's independence,
b) to save nagging the child to 'hurry up'
c) to save some of the repetition which can be harrowing for all of the family.

NB A dog can be a wonderful source of comfort when 'nobody else understands'. I'm sure parents will say, 'I've enough to do without a dog', but the dog will listen to secrets and hurts that can't be revealed to anyone else; won't object to being cried on; won't make judgments when things go wrong and will always know the way home. And of course the child with dyspraxia can be given the responsibility of looking out for the dog and 'being in charge', which can be a novel and uplifting experience. A dog can even guard a child when he has to be left alone.

Checklists

Before school	Preparing for school	At school	Home and evening	Going to bed
Getting up 1. Find slippers (easiest on a plain carpet) and dressing gown 2. Toilet 3. Wash 4. Go downstairs 5. Let dog out 6. Have breakfast (cereal then toast) 7. Go upstairs and brush teeth	1. Get dressed (follow code) 2. Pack schoolbag • pencil case • books • PE kit • money for bus 3. Pack lunchbox • sandwich • drink • apple • crisps	1. Cloakroom • put coat on peg • undo bag • take pencil and books to class • give money to teacher 2. Hand in homework 3. Collect silent reading book 4. Check tray for returned work	1. Put shoes and coat ready for for morning 2. Change into play clothes 3. Have a snack 4. Play with dog outside 5. Watch TV 6. Homework 7. Supper	1. Shirt and pants to the wash 2. Clean teeth 3. Get washed 4. Put pyjamas on 5. Go downstairs (slippers and dressing gown) 6. Say goodnight 7. Go to bed

Numbers can be covered with plastic and have blu tack or velcro to fix/detach them to a board. They can be re-used as appropriate.

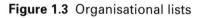

Figure 1.3 Organisational lists

CHAPTER 2

Studying dyspraxia within a developmental framework

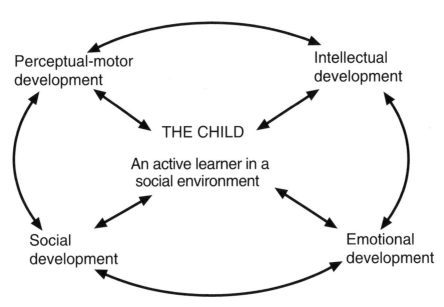

Figure 2.1 The interplay of different aspects of development

The study of dyspraxia and that of child development complement each other naturally. The patterns of developmental change are the same for all children in every culture, although the rate at which they pass through the stages and their ultimate level of 'achievement', be that motor or intellectual, is different. This means that developmental norms, i.e. the set of statistics which show what 'normal' expectations of children at different ages are, can be set and the achievements of children with dyspraxia can be compared to them, thus giving a reliable way of estimating the impact which dyspraxia has. This gives a clearer picture than the 'hunch' that something is wrong. Dividing the study of development into separate aspects is somewhat artificial because progress, or indeed regression, in one impinges on all of the others, however it is helpful to have a structure which can make this complex study more manageable! The one suggested here, is to subdivide the study of development into four aspects, namely:

- Social development – or the study of how children build relationships and learn to interact in groups;
- Perceptual-motor development – or the study of how children learn to move efficiently and effectively in different environments;
- Intellectual development – or the study of how children learn to be logical and rational thinkers;
- Emotional development – or the study of how children's feelings and perceptions affect their behaviour and learning.

Of course, all children are active in constructing the way they react to the environmental benefits and pressures. This makes the study fascinating, difficult and often unpredictable! Personality factors affect the way different children respond – some overcome huge disadvantages to have happy, fulfilled lives, while others, with apparently much more going for them, succumb at the least hurdle and achieve much less than their circumstances would seem to predict. This is the same for children with dyspraxia. Children with the same level of difficulty react differently – resilient children will see more opportunities, make the most of them and cope, while more vulnerable children will need a great deal of support for a longer period of time. Still, whether children have a specific difficulty or not, changes in one aspect of development, e.g. through growth or intellectual development or changing family circumstances, impinge on all of the others and the total picture can only emerge when all of these interactions have been considered.

Example

After a long struggle Tom learned to swim. Both Tom and all his family were delighted by his progress. But what had he gained?

Well first of all and most obviously, he had taken a huge stride forward, mainly in the perceptual-motor domain, but this progress also spilled over into the other aspects of his development. For now that he was able to swim, he could stay with his friends in the pool and interact with them. This was an important social gain which would hopefully give him the confidence to build relationships with these other children in different settings. And as Tom gained confidence in the water, he was probably interested to discover the names of different strokes, where they were best used and the kinds of physical demands which were needed to perform them. This was an intellectual gain. Possibly best of all, Tom had become more confident in his own ability to learn a new skill and this, enhancing his self-esteem, was a vital emotional gain.

It is particularly important to recognise the spinoffs and give lots of praise when children with dyspraxia make progress, because their achievement will have taken a great deal of effort.

It would also be helpful to point out to the child that he will be able to use this new skill in different settings, maybe to explaining to Tom that he will now be able to swim in the sea and in other swimming pools, for example. Although this may seem over the top, Rush (1997) tells of one child who learned to swim and then asked her teacher, 'Now will you teach me to swim in my pool?' This child had no understanding that her new skill could transfer to a different environment. This very bright and articulate child thought she would have to learn all over again! And so a moment's thought and explanation can help transfer of learning and prevent all sorts of worries.

This is why Figure 2.1 has arrows linking the different subdivisions of development. They are to remind those who observe children, assess their progress and plan learning activities on that basis, that progress in one area is likely to benefit other areas as well. In similar vein, new or unhappy experiences can cause children to regress to an earlier developmental stage, and then they will appear unable to do something which they had mastered before. This explains why parents can be flummoxed to find that their five-year-old youngster, successfully toilet-trained for some considerable time, has been having accidents in his new school. Perhaps the child has forgotten where the toilets are (did anyone show him?) or stiff new buttonholes defeated fumbling fingers, or the child, unsure of attempting a first-time visit, simply waited for too long before going to the toilet at all. Once confidence is regained through simple but appropriate measures being taken (elastic instead of buttons, clear directions to the toilet with a large red arrow as a reminder, even asking the children, 'Who wants to go?') some of the problems can disappear!

Even at the top of the school, some children, particularly those with dyspraxia, can find new experiences daunting. Outings from home or from school can cause panic because a whole set of possible disasters loom. 'Treats' such as a class outing, which other children anticipate with joy, mean uncertainty and breaks in a safe routine and appear full of new and unwelcome challenges: 'Where will we go? How long will the journey take? What is going to happen?'. Lots of 'What ifs' which translate into lots of worries. If the children have difficulty in following sequences of instructions, or in recognising time frames, e.g. how long something takes or lasts, explanations such as, 'We'll go on the bus, then we'll go to the cafe for lunch then I'll tell you about the afternoon, and reassurances', e.g. that the information desk where the children are to meet after their free time is clearly sign posted as are the toilets, can prevent the children being fearful of losing sight of the teacher and help them to relax and enjoy their day. Some children will also need to know that 'We won't leave till everyone is back', if free time is part of the plan. If this doesn't happen and if the plans are too confusing, children may realise they can't cope and resort to bad behaviour or having a sore tummy – anything which means they don't have to go. Those who don't understand the children's fears will see only the avoidance tactics, but if the children don't go, they miss all the learning, both intellectual and social, their vulnerability is exposed to all their peers and this may result in the children being ridiculed. Sadly, bullying happens quite often with these children.

What can be done to help?

Rehearsing what will happen is often helpful, especially when boundaries or safety strategies are to be explained. The children could be very relieved to know that 'no-one will be allowed to go far from the teachers', or that paths or streets are easy to follow. Those in charge must decentre, i.e. put themselves in the place of fearful children and try to anticipate the kinds of worries they will have.

Recording observations and assessments

As the different aspects of development interact, often in quite subtle ways, it can be difficult to know where to record different assessments.

In my view, considering progress across the spectrum and weighing up all the advantages is more important than worrying about recording observations in the 'correct' place. In fact, different viewpoints can form the basis of rich discussions about the children's progress.

Example

If a child is able to get dressed after PE in an acceptable amount of time now (where previously that was really difficult), what kind of progress is that? Is it intellectual? (the child can now understand the order of putting clothes on and gauge the time to be spent on each action), is it perceptual-motor? (the child has now developed the coordination to be able to do up buttons and tie laces), or is it emotional? (the child has gained confidence from not being last).

The children themselves can put greatest value on the less obvious benefits – 'When I can swim, I'll be allowed to go to the pool on my own!' Craig is anxious to be independent and free – and when he can manage to do this, he will have made a huge social and emotional step forward. But success will depend on intellectual and motor competence too, for the child will have to remember 'what bus' and how to cope in the dressing rooms, where to find the wrist band and how to put it on. Thinking through the organisation of going swimming makes us realise just what a complex task it is.

A more detailed look at the rationale for choosing these aspects of development as key contributors to learning now follows.

Social development

Many parents and teachers would say that the social dimension of learning is the most important one, because if children are happy in school, they are likely to be more receptive and confident and therefore more able to take new learning on board – or at least they will not be afraid to ask for help. Moreover, sociable children are able to interact and learn from their peer group as well as from their parents and teachers. Many important researchers emphasise the importance of active children learning in a social setting. Vygotsky's (1978) concept of 'the zone of proximal development' and Bruner's (1966) idea of 'scaffolding' both claim that if children are supported by more knowledgeable others as they learn, and these need only be one step ahead, they will be able to move forward more quickly than if they tried to learn alone.

Social development is therefore vitally important as it enables children to

- build relationships with others,
- learn from others,
- interact appropriately with adults and children,
- cooperate in group situations,
- take the lead role in decision making,
- take the subsidiary role at times,
- become aware that others have needs too,
- learn to empathise, i.e. understand different perspectives,
- understand how events affect others,
- develop socially acceptable behaviour in different circumstances,
- make decisions (social and/or moral) and stay with them,
- appreciate the value of friendship, and
- develop altruism, i.e. caring for others at some cost to oneself.

The list, however, shows where children with dyspraxia are unable to comply, for they often find it very difficult to build relationships beyond the family group. This is not really surprising given that these others are not likely to recognise their difficulties. Or perhaps their difficulties in social situations spring from a general lack of confidence in their own ability to tackle new things and possibly lay themselves open to further disappointment and so they stay close to those they know will offer support. Another social difficulty comes from an inherent block in being able to empathise with others. Dyspraxic children seem unable to appreciate another person's success or realise that they are unhappy. Perhaps this is because they have to concentrate so hard on overcoming their own difficulties, or perhaps they don't want to 'look outwards and see' because then they realise that others are managing better than they are – at least in movement tasks. Giving lots of (deserved) praise in activities such as oral story telling or computer work or mathematical reasoning, i.e. in whatever the children do well, will hopefully boost these children so that they can accept their limitations and cooperate in trying to overcome them. Again this is a case of one kind of progress helping another.

Perceptual-motor development

The perceptual-motor aspects of development concern the acquisition of practical skills through developing abilities such as coordination, balance, strength and speed of movement. The underlying skills of planning movements so that they are efficient and effective, involve much perceptual learning based on making spatial and kinaesthetic decisions. These depend on the other senses – visual, auditory and tactile – and on interpreting environmental cues accurately, so that feedback into the sensory system guides decisions about when to move, what to move and where to go.

Example

Let's find how acquisition of one of the early movement patterns impacts on the different aspects of development. Let's look at crawling, usually a favourite way of getting around by about nine months. This is an important stage in development yet parents not understanding the inherent learning within crawling can be pleased when this stage is missed out. But why should it be missed? The strange thing is that children who don't crawl, very often can't crawl. As a result they lack early sequencing and coordination practice, and experience in stretching forward and making spatial decisions, such as how far and in which direction, while they are in a secure position. Picture a child in a prone kneeling position, ready to crawl. Imagine one hand stretching

---

forward to go into the movement. As this happens, the body weight must shift to be completely supported by the other three points. This is good practice for learning to balance. If children don't experience this, they are missing out a fundamental stage in learning to move effectively in different environments, for balance is essential to stability both in stillness and in movement, i.e. in being able to stand well balanced and secure with postural control (static balance), and with the body held steady with equal strength on both sides of the body in a forward roll (dynamic balance).

It is interesting and informative to discover that many children who haven't crawled have reading difficulties, sometimes dyslexia. One reason is because they have missed out on sequencing practice, i.e. moving limbs in the correct order and so imprinting a pattern of sequential movement into the brain. But most often, not being able to crawl is an early sign of dyspraxia.

It is important that due attention is given to perceptual-motor development because this enables children to:

- control their movements with increasing dexterity;
- move effectively and safely in different environments;
- develop spatial and kinesthetic awareness;
- develop the abilities that underlie skilled performance;
- know how to organise sequences of movement;
- become involved in health giving activities;
- enjoy participating in sports, gymnastics and dance; and
- be confident in tackling new movement challenges.

This is the aspect of development that dyspraxic children find particularly problematic and many heartrending stories are told when children aren't allowed to play. 'I want to try to play football', cried David, 'but they'll only let me be a goal post – for 45 minutes too – it's not fair.' And indeed, it isn't fair at all. The natural thing is for children to avoid situations like this – not all children would be as forceful as David was – and of course this prevents them having practice. However, the pros and cons must be carefully weighed up, and if a vulnerable child is being made unhappy, then a substitute activity or a specially designed perceptual-motor programme is the child's right. Examples of activities and programmes are in Chapter 8 and in the appendices of this book.

Intellectual development

The intellectual or cognitive aspects of development concern the acquisition of knowledge and understanding about all aspects of everyday life and in all areas of the curriculum. Children need to develop this so that they can learn:

- to develop knowledge and understanding of the world;
- to develop language and communication skills;
- to develop the capacity to think logically and rationally;
- to make informed decisions;
- to develop mathematical and scientific concepts;
- to solve problems;
- to think creatively about new ways of doing things;
- to concentrate on the task at hand; and
- to cope with specialised learning in the classroom and at home.

This last item concerns the classroom. Children with dyspraxia are bright and have little trouble with intellectual tasks, however when learning has to be demonstrated through some kind of movement, then difficulties may become apparent. The technical aspects of writing may be problematic due to poor control of the pencil. The tendency to scribe letters back to front, due to poor laterality, or the short term memory problem may cause children to forget how the letters are formed. Sequencing difficulties may hamper storytelling as retaining the order of the tale – knowing that the beginning or introduction comes before the middle or main input and that the story must logically progress to the end – is quite taxing. Dyspraxic children often have marked success with oral work because then they can give their imaginations full play and/or solve problems which take quite sophisticated reasoning although writing them down just couldn't happen. Perhaps they could tape-record their stories and transcribe them later? The benefit of this is that the tape can be replayed and paused and this takes away the strain of memorising the story and so it can be written, part by part, on different 'good' days.

If dyspraxic children have aspects of dyslexia, and 50 per cent of them do, reading will be problematic and this can confuse 'markers' into thinking that the underlying concepts of the lesson have not been understood. Using simple words to convey instructions or substituting symbols or pictures or text can be very helpful, depending on the age of the children. The computer is a great boon as children can record their stories, even in conjunction with an audio tape, and then the spell checker can help to reduce mistakes and enhance the chances of success.

In all parts of the curriculum, it is important that the lessons are prepared to take account of the individual children's difficulties and although this is time consuming at the start, soon the rewards for both children and teachers outweigh the time spent. In music lessons, for example, children can be encouraged to select an instrument to match their capabilities – something sturdy like an Orff Xylophone would suit a child who has difficulty gauging the strength needed to play with any kind of finesse. Like the computer, the child can manage playing the xylophone, because hands can stay on their own side of the body. Once the child gains confidence, then crossing the midline and more delicate playing can be encouraged. A moment's sympathetic planning can spare a child the humiliation of breaking an instrument and possibly having to endure the jeers of his classmates.

Emotional development

This is perhaps the most difficult area to understand, possibly because the development of confidence, as one example, is only apparent in carrying out another task or perhaps in changed non-verbal behaviour, for example the gait, i.e. the carriage and the poise in walking. Non-verbal behaviour is always difficult to assess accurately as facial expressions can be very misleading, although lots of teachers will claim to know what is going on inside a child's head. 'I'd be a funny kind of teacher if I couldn't tell if he was trying or not,' said one teacher, but personally I'm never so sure! Often involving the children's own spoken evaluations is a safer bet. Other things like appreciation or imagination are less tangible than getting a sum right and making progress in mathematics, and this makes assessment problematic, but this is a hugely important aspect of development for it allows children to:

- pretend to be someone else;
- approach new situations with confidence;
- express feelings and emotions;
- cope with anxieties and be more resilient;
- enjoy open-ended problems;
- appreciate works of art/music/dance;
- cry if they want to;
- understand the perception of other people;
- develop altruism;
- appreciate the atmosphere in e.g. a church;
- be innovative and imaginative.

Again aspects of this can be difficult for dyspraxic children who don't decentre, in that they don't readily understand the perceptions or standpoints of others or their points of view. This makes it difficult for children to play together. Observers must distinguish between children playing in parallel, i.e. two children playing alongside each other but with no common purpose and no interaction, and play where the children act together to devolve some imaginative ploy or build a model or discuss plans.

But why should these children have this problem? Children with dyspraxia often can't read other children's non-verbal signals and so they make inappropriate responses such as laughing loudly when the game needs them to be quiet. And because they find judging distances difficult, they tend to intrude into another child's personal space. The other child can feel threatened by this, and especially if it happens with a bang and a clatter (due to lack of judgment in how much speed to use), they shy away. The dyspraxic child immediately feels rejected and hurt, without knowing how he offended.

Linked to the difficulty in following instructions, the children with dyspraxia often find it difficult to follow the rules of a game. So many childhood games have unwritten 'rules' and it is difficult for parents to understand what is going on and therefore impossible to rehearse them with their child. But the other children know these rules, seemingly without any explanation, and the dyspraxic child, not understanding, infringes them and is blamed for spoiling the game.

Example

Listen to Irene, Paul's Mum. She explained,
   'When Paul developed this great interest in his train set, I was so relieved and I thought, "now is the time to ask two other boys in his class to tea". I thought that if they got to know Paul at home and had a nice time, then at school they would let him play. Before the boys arrived, Paul and I talked about sharing and taking turns and that was fine. On reflection, however, I realised that he had rehearsed what would happen too much. At first all was well, but when the boys wanted to change the route the trains ran and so alter the game, Paul couldn't cope. He got agitated and shouted, "They're not playing the right way – they've got to go home." So they did. Later, when we had calmed down, I realised that was what I often said to Paul, "If you aren't good, we'll have to go home."'
   Obviously distressed, Irene asked, 'How do you explain all the nuances of social behaviour to a child with dyspraxia?'

Another difficulty arises if the child takes every utterance, every plan, every story literally.

Example

Colin explained, 'We have to be so careful how we tell Jake about things we might do. One year we had promised that when we went on holiday he could swim in the sea. When we arrived at St Andrews, the mist was well in over the sea and the beach was deserted, but Jake couldn't be persuaded to wait. "You promised, you promised," he yelled and we had to let him bathe. He couldn't understand that he'd have a better time later when the sun came through. It had to be now because he had interpreted "When we go on holiday" as "the very minute we arrive!" Jake can't cope with any change in plan. Everything has to be by the book!'

Example

Hannah's teacher spoke about her wonderful stories and her enjoyment of any time when creative thinking was to be shared. While this was a real bonus for Hannah and the class, she was also very concerned about the level of Hannah's immersion in her fantasy world. 'When Hannah tells about being a fairy, she becomes one – she would eat leaves and berries because that's what fairies eat.' And so the teacher had constantly to watch in case the child was harmed. 'Hannah loves to dream', she explained, 'and sometimes it's quite a thought to pull her back to a harsher world.'

This gives another insight into the thinking of a child with dyspraxia and helps explain the responsibilities which parents and teachers have in keeping their children safe.

Coping with children with dyspraxia is challenging and complex, made even more difficult by the fact that the children at the centre of it all are not passive recipients, but people who make decisions and react to teaching and other forms of intervention in their own way. The Scottish Consultative Council on the Curriculum (1999) agrees, explaining that,

Each child is an unique individual. Each brings a different life story to the school setting. Growing up as a member of a family and community with unique ways of understanding the world creates an individual pattern and pace of development.

And so children bring their own richness to learning through sharing their experiences and interests. Generally speaking, they are greatly influenced by their family's attitude to education; after all, parents are the children's first educators; they are the ones who provide the early experiences and the early cultural impact. And as learning is eased if the children can build on something that is familiar to them, those who teach have to recognise and respect the children's previous learning, their cultural environment and the quality and quantity of the opportunities they have had. Then there is their genetic endowment which plays an important part, for some children will have a greater capacity to do well in school terms, than others. But of course ability alone does not ensure success and less able children are often able to work hard and shine. All the genetic and environmental influences work together to give each child a unique profile. The contribution of each has long been debated. The conclusion has usually been that a constant and complex interplay determines the child's behaviour. Is this different when children have dyspraxia?

Heredity and environment

When parents discover that their child has a difficulty such as dyspraxia, they are usually anxious to know 'What has caused this? Is it inherited? Did we do something wrong, perhaps give the wrong food or not give enough attention?' The first important point to emphasise is that dyspraxia can happen to anyone and no one should feel inadequate or guilty. The question of whether dyspraxia is inherited is being investigated to find whether a specific gene can be identified. In the absence of scientific evidence it is interesting to hear what parents say. Parents of children with dyspraxia often endorse the genetic stance. They say, 'Yes, he's just like his uncle', or 'a cousin is having the same kinds of difficulties', or 'she's just like her mum', observations which would seem to point to a genetic source. However, reflection isn't always dependable and if these relations are older than the child, the condition may not have been diagnosed. Dyspraxia may not even have been recognised at that time and so there will be no record more accurate than hearsay!

In similar vein, and although parents are sometimes nervous about asking, there have been no proven links between difficulties in pregnancy or early attachment problems and subsequent dyspraxia. Yet from the start, some parents know there is something wrong. Perhaps the baby is floppy, with poor muscle tone, or he has difficulty feeding due to the coordination required in sucking or perhaps the baby is tetchy and irritable or a poor sleeper, one who never seems to be at peace. Parents themselves often blame birth trauma, particularly anoxia (deprivation of oxygen to the baby during the birth process) and there are some researchers, e.g. Cotrell (1992), who argue that this *is* the case.

Parents, worn out by trying to comfort their child, may need outside help or medication and they can feel so inadequate and disappointed that the relationship with their child is not what they had envisaged. One young mum who had anticipated lots of fun and reciprocal love explained, 'I wanted her to love me. She is all I have, but she didn't, she just cried and cried and when I could take no more, I hit her'. This was an extreme case but many exhausted parents will understand how a poor environment and a crying baby just broke the mum down. Parents must be able to get help long before that point is reached for the wellbeing of all the family. A difficult start may also prevent secure bonding, which can have enduring negative effects (Ainsworth 1972). But of course not all dyspraxic children have early problems, and many families cope very well. Some difficulties don't become apparent until fine motor skills are required. Then parents worry that they have missed early signs. The key thing is for parents to ask, no *insist* that they have access to specialist help as soon as difficulties are identified and seem to be more than temporary blips that could be due to the children being off colour.

A study of the effects of maternal diet on a baby in the first four weeks has been reported by Lucas *et al.* (1992). This showed that for pre-term and small for dates babies, those fed on breast milk showed significant advantages in terms of IQ at age eight. The advantage came from DHA (docoahexanoic), a long chain fatty acid which is beneficial in the maternal diet and for the first four weeks of the baby's life. Ongoing research is concerned with the metabolism of fatty acids and this may show that additions to the diet such as evening primrose oil or fish oil can help some children. Some parents reported immediate improvement in their children's coordination. It is essential, however, that any dietary additions are overseen by the child's doctor as some children react badly to them. Kirby (1999b) explains that children with epilepsy can be made worse, and this may be true for other children as well, so care must be taken until more investigations have been completed.

How do parents cope?

Parents' reactions to the diagnosis of dyspraxia are very different. Lots of parents are very distressed because everyone wants their children not to have problems, yet others seem to take it in their stride and say, 'Right, where do we go from here?' Many are relieved to have a specific diagnosis, although some paediatricians can be reluctant to give it. As one parent explained, "Why worry about giving the child a label . . . surely the label, "Dyspraxia" is much better than being told your child is lazy, which is what I've been told again and again'. And for those who are Scots, one hugely smiling and totally unconcerned mum told me, 'Och, he's just like his faither, gallus!' The lad seemed to accept his limitations with the same good humour, even though he sometimes 'got clouted for breaking things!' Giving these different examples is intended to comfort parents that they are not alone and to show that there are different ways of reacting, depending possibly on the personality factors of the parents and children, the expectations they have, the resources at their disposal and very importantly, the quality and quantity of help that is at hand.

Perhaps just knowing that there are others who are finding it difficult to cope and offering to meet them to exchange tactics can help; perhaps asking families and friends to give parents a short but regular break can be a life-saver; perhaps even saying, 'it will be better when there are more choices for the child so that his difficulties are not always on display', can help too. A most important move is to build the kind of relationship with the teacher which allows parents to explain in a calm way the difficulties the child has and to suggest ways in which he could be helped. If these can be coping ways in the first instance, the teachers are more likely to welcome suggestions for teaching ways later. Concentrating on the things the child can do, not what siblings could do at the same age, and constantly and consistently praising all the children in the family is the best way. Teachers are always advised to 'catch them being good and praise them'. It's a maxim that rarely fails. In the last resort parents need to remember that there are children who are much more severely disabled. This in no way detracts from the difficulties dyspraxic children have, but it does help to keep them in proportion. (Lists of support groups are in Appendix 5.)

And of course the question of whether the parents have enough information to be able to judge how they should react is important too. Many parents complain that no one has explained what they can do to relieve their children's difficulties. Perhaps this is because of the complexity of the different possible problems which are not evident in every child or perhaps it is because of the difficulty of making prognoses about how different children will develop and to what extent they can be helped. Children can surprise by how much they can achieve and this is as true of dyspraxic children as any other, although it may take longer and need more effort. Very often, short spells of regular practice can give amazing results, but parents and teachers have to be sensitive as to the best time, i.e. not when the children are too tired for that is self-defeating. Finding something the child is really interested in and then having short regular private practices until the child feels confident to 'go public' and give everyone a surprise, is often a good way forward!

The question of how parents react to their children's difficulties will obviously affect how the children cope and this brings in the question of environmental influences. All children need lots of love and support but the children with dyspraxia who tend to be isolates need their security reinforced more than the others. Unfortunately, they can vent their frustrations on the very ones who are helping them most and this causes great distress to the parents and to the children themselves who know that this is the worst thing they can do, but can't stop.

Example

One dad explained, 'Eventually, I got totally exasperated by Graeme's tantrums and bursts of rage, and so I went to our GP and explained that although Graeme was doing a bit better socially at school, at home living with him was grim. The doctor said that his behaviour was a compliment to us because he knew we would stand by him no matter what – he felt that his home was a secure place to release his frustrations. What could I say? And we wouldn't have considered drugs, not that they were offered, so it looks as if we'll just have to soldier on and be thankful that school life is a bit more manageable for him.'

The process of getting enough help and support is important and one which causes much relief or much anguish. At school, some children have a computer, an auxiliary and a daily perceptual-motor programme, while others have much less help. One child was given a laptop which had a tiny screen. This meant he could not see what he had written beyond the few visible words and so his sentence structure didn't make any kind of sense. The keyboard was also too small to allow him to type with any degree of accuracy and the frustrations caused by the 'help' were unbearable and unnecessary. The response to the agitated parent was, 'He's bright – he'll manage, I have others who need much more help'. And while we all understand the huge pressures teachers have, this kind of justification doesn't help the dyspraxic child or the family to cope.

Personality and temperament

One aspect of development which is claimed to be linked to heredity is temperament. Children seem to inherit temperamental traits which affect their behaviour. Two sets which are particularly applicable to children with dyspraxia are impulsiveness <————> reflection and vulnerability <————> resilience. Doubters might ask how researchers can be sure, given that from the moment they are born, children have role models in their parents. Will they not then copy what they see? Evidence for the 'nature' against the 'nurture' claim is that two children brought up by the same parents in the same environment can be 'chalk and cheese!' One might be quicksilver, acting before thinking and landing in all sorts of scrapes (the impulsive one), while the other child was reflective, carefully weighing up the consequences of doing something and making a considered decision before acting at all.

Then there is the child who is sensitive and easily hurt, the child who gets bullied because he retreats from any confrontation. He is the vulnerable one. His brother however, shrugs off barbs and arrows and lives to fight another day. Resilient children usually have an easier time of it in everyday dealings and they also tend to see and grasp opportunities which pass the less confident child by. Certainly the sunny-natured child appears to have long-lasting advantages over the more sombre one. Garmezy (1993) explains, saying 'vulnerable children are open to the worst stresses of childhood while others [i.e. the resilient ones] are buffeted from the worst consequences'.

But if these traits are inherited, what happens if the child inherits 'shyness' from one parent and 'outgoingness' from the other? What then? Bee (1999) explains that typically, one gene will be dominant and this will influence the child's behaviour while the other is recessive and will have no effect. However the recessive gene may emerge again in a later generation. Hence the comments, 'He's just Grandpa all over again!'

These temperamental traits however, are open to environmental modification.

Example

If a child inherits the temperamental trait 'impulsiveness' and so tends to act without considering the consequences, then a home and school setting which models 'slowing down' and thinking through the outcomes of actions could be very salutary. If, for example, adults help the child practise 'crossing the road drill', calmly pointing out the dangers, then later the child may be less likely to dive into the road. Of course, one example won't do much to change usual ways of behaving. Constant and consistent examples are needed to influence temperamental traits which house relatively enduring characteristics. For although children may well learn to slow down in familiar situations, when new ones arise, they tend to instinctively respond in their own temperamental way. Impulsivity does tend to diminish somewhat as children mature – this can be seen when they require less supervision and 'get out to play'. Children with dyspraxia, however, often retain a high level of impulsivity so no one can take any chances that they will be safe. They need extended supervision which can place a strain on everyone concerned!

Growth and maturation

The idea that both the equipment and the learning environment should 'fit' the developing child highlights the issue of growth and the related concept, maturation, i.e. the two remaining influences on development.

'Growth' is a description of quantitive change. The word is most often used to refer to physical growth, but it is really quite a wide term encompassing things like growing vocabulary, growth in skill, in dexterity or logical thinking, growing responsibility or growing independence. All children in all cultures pass through the same patterns of change. Physical development is cephalocaudal (i.e. progressing from head to toe), and proximodistal, (i.e. progressing from the centre to the periphery). This is why babies can hold their heads up before their back muscles are strong enough to let them sit and why they can sit before they are able to pull up to stand. Most children crawl, even up stairs, before they walk, for crawling and climbing depend on the same action! The instructions for these sequences are built in at the moment of conception, they are not taught. Even anxious parents can't teach their children to walk. They won't walk till they are 'ready', till they have the strength and balance and coordination, i.e. the maturity, to allow them to try. The fact that most children walk between 11 and 18 months establishes one detail in a timetable of age-norms and this is often used as an assessment device to measure progress. It must be remembered however, that the span of 'normal' development is wide.

Physical growth in dyspraxic children is no different to the pattern which other children follow; they are just as tall and their body parts are all in proportion. They meet the growth norms, or size expectations set by chronological age. The children with poor muscle tone however, will lack strength and this prevents them being able to match the norm in tasks like writing, which is often messy and difficult to read. Lack of strength in the shoulders and/or fingers results in little pencil control. Nor are they able to kick a ball if the lack of strength is in the pelvic region and legs, for this affects stability and balance and possibly mobility. This means that the children are not able to do the movement skills expected of them by their families, teachers and peer group. They do not meet the expectations indicated by their appearance. And because children in particular value physical prowess highly, and because the demonstration of any movement is public, the children who 'can't do' have a miserable experience which impacts negatively on their self-esteem.

Verbal dyspraxia

When children have poor muscle tone in the mouth which affects coordination in the speech apparatus, they are said to have verbal dyspraxia. Usually they are very late in developing speech at all and may offer no words till they are three years old and then stay with single words for a considerable time. Poor coordination makes articulation difficult and speech incomprehensible. It can be very distressing for the child not to be understood although sometimes other children can communicate when adults fail. For older children, speaking in front of their peer group becomes impossible, the children stay mute and this can confuse teachers into thinking that their vocabulary is slow to develop. Given speech therapy to help with articulation and then time and encouragement to build up confidence, these children can demonstrate that they have a comprehensive, even imaginative repertoire of words. Parents often need to help a new teacher understand this, for after all they will have 30 or so other children, all with their own sets of difficulties and demands.

Signs of verbal dyspraxia:

- difficulty in making speech sounds;
- difficulty in ordering sounds to make words;
- difficulty in sustaining the quality of produced speech; and
- difficulty in controlling the rhythm and loudness of speech.

The fact that dyspraxic children are likely to be just as tall and well built as the others may have one disadvantage and that is due, once more, to teachers' expectations of children who are big. Research, e.g. by Lerner (1985), shows that teachers tend to expect big children to cope in a more responsible manner, i.e. they are misled by visual cues, often overlooking the children's chronological age and coping ability. This can negatively affect dyspraxic children who struggle with organisation and planning. They have enough to do to cope with themselves and are not really able to accept more responsibility or look out for others as well. And so there is an important psychological aspect to growth which needs to be considered.

Maturation

While 'growth' describes the developmental changes which occur over time, 'maturation' explains them. The term means 'the genetically programmed patterns of change which begin at conception and continue till death' (Gessell 1925). These patterns are inbuilt and untutored. After all, no one teaches a child to laugh or cry or even walk. The effects of neurological and physical maturation can be seen as children become more skilled in coping, i.e. in planning, organising and doing whatever it is they choose to do.

Early motor development

Picture a baby lying in a cot with a mobile just above. The baby is excited to see it, but although she watches it closely, almost without blinking, she makes no movement towards it. In the same situation a month later, the baby can be seen to make a whole range of uncoordinated movements in response to trying to reach it – facial grimaces show the effort involved – but, although arms and legs are flailing, the purpose of the activity, i.e. getting hold of the toy, is not achieved. During that activity however, the child's hand may strike the toy and gradually she realises that she has some control over her arm. She now knows she can cause things to happen. She is now involved in a problem-solving activity, 'How do I get it again?' and after many tries her movements become more refined and accurate until at about four months she can look and reach and grasp, a sophisticated and purposeful set of actions. She has still to work out how to let go – a much more difficult feat! What, then has the child learned?

1. That her actions cause things to happen, i.e. she can be in control.
2. That there is a difference between herself and the object out there. She learns where she ends and the outside world begins, i.e. her body boundary.
3. When to stretch and where to stretch, i.e. how far and in what direction.
4. What happens to the rest of her body when she moves one part, i.e. kinesthetic awareness.

5. That her successes will be applauded by those watching, i.e. she learns to redo movements which win praise and through that build secure social relationships. This promotes confidence as well as competence in the movement itself.

These are very important developmental gains, primarily in the perceptual-motor field, but confidence in being able to be successful stimulates development in the emotional domain, for those who watch and encourage help her to know that adults will approve her efforts and this enables her to try other things. As the child internalises or habituates a successful movement pattern, she finds that successive 'shots' don't require the same amount of effort. The early thinking and planning as well as the 'learning to do' have been internalised and can be called upon again when a similar movement is required.

The child learns to adapt a learned movement to fit another situation and so a repertoire of increasingly complex actions is built up. Ayres (1972) explains that children with dyspraxia find this adaptation or transfer of learning very difficult. They don't seem to recognise the similarities in patterns and so it takes longer for them to do unaccustomed movements. Through practice they manage habitual movements or everyday movements reasonably well, but new movements can be very difficult; they have to be planned as a first time try. But what kind of maturation allows this to occur? What happens to allow children to develop increasingly skilled movement?

Neurological maturation

At birth the midbrain and medulla are most fully developed (Figure 2.2). These two parts, which are in the lower brain and are connected to the spinal cord, respond to 'survival demands', e.g. hunger and fear, and regulate basic tasks such as sleeping and waking and giving attention – all things which newborns can do. The least well developed part is the cortex, the convoluted grey matter that wraps around the midbrain and controls perception and language and body movement – all the complex thinking and doing scenarios. All of these structures are composed of two basic types of cells, glial cells and neurones. Glial cells form the 'glue' that holds the system together. They keep the brain firm and so protect the delicate structures. They also help to remove debris from dying or injured cells. They develop at about 13 weeks after conception and are added till the child is about two years of age.

The neurones or nerve cells begin to appear about 12 weeks after conception and are all present by about 28 weeks (Figure 2.3). They have an electrical and chemical function that enables them to transmit messages along a one-way connection tube called the axon which is gradually covered by a protective coating (myelination) to

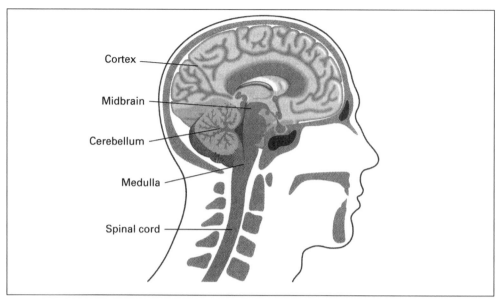

Figure 2.2 The main structures of the brain

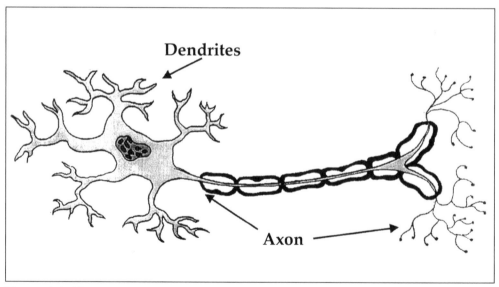

Figure 2.3 Neurones

insulate it and protect it from other connective tissue. In some children, myelination is not complete till age six or so, and this can affect these children's coordination skills. The timing of this process also helps to explain why paediatricians are reluctant to make early diagnoses of dyspraxia or developmental coordination disorder, for ongoing myelination may reduce some of the coordination difficulties. It may help to realise that in multiple sclerosis the myelin sheath is breaking down, causing sufferers to lose control of their movements. This is the reverse of the maturation process.

In the cerebral cortex of the brain, millions and millions of these neurones or nerve cells respond to external stimuli from the senses: sight, hearing, smell, touch and kinesthesis or awareness of where the body is in space.

These neurones have four important parts:

1. a cell body;
2. dendrites or branchlike extensions from the cell body which are the main receptors of nerve impulses;
3. the axon which is a tubular extension of the cell body; and
4. terminal fibres at the end of the axon which form the primary transmitting apparatus of the nervous system.

(Bee 1995)

Bee explains that the branchlike appearance of the dendrites has caused psychologists to use botanical language to describe their function. They talk of the 'dendritic arbor' and 'pruning' of the arbor. What do they mean?

In the early embryonic period, axons are short and there is little development of the dendrites. But in the last two months before birth and in the first years after, there is massive activity. The dendritic arbor occurs and this provides the vast number of synapses necessary for the brain and body to function together. A synapse is the point at which the transmitting fibres from the axon come into close contact with another neurone's dendrites. It is the point where the instructions for action are passed from one neurone to the next. Electrical activity coming from the axon of one neurone releases a chemical, a neurotransmitter, and this stimulates electrical activity in another. This can happen between nerve cells and others such as muscle cells. There are vast numbers of synapses which involves huge growth in the dendritic arbor and the weight of the brain triples in the first two years.

This development, however, is not smooth and continuous, for some of the vast number of pathways which have been formed are superfluous and by the time the children are three or so, many of the pathways which have not been involved in useful actions will have been pruned. Experience, therefore, does not add new pathways but causes redundant or extra ones to disappear.

Think back to the baby in the cot wanting to have the toy, but producing only random, uncoordinated, purposeless movements. At this stage, there are far too many messages being transmitted to all four limbs and these prevent effective movement taking place and only serve to confuse the system. But when successful action is practised, in this case when the child manages to grasp the toy, then the pathways and connections used to achieve that action are reinforced. The redundant ones are eliminated and the 'wiring diagram' is cleaned up (Greenough, Black and Wallace 1987). When the system is pruned like this, information from the senses can be transmitted efficiently because there are fewer unproductive alternatives, fewer choices about where to go!

What then causes dyspraxia?

Following the description of neurological development outlined above, it seems that dyspraxic children have fewer reinforced interconnections and so the cortex remains in a state of immaturity (Portwood 1998). And so messages which should only go to one limb go to all four. If the child wishes to reach out to lift a cup perhaps, then the other arm will stretch forward too, and if the child is asked to walk along a straight line on his heels (an assessment test), his arms will be raised in front of him without him being aware that this has occurred. These superfluous actions use extra time and energy and may prevent two hands or two feet being used together to do different things, such as holding paper in one hand and cutting with scissors with the other, or standing on one foot and kicking a ball with the other.

Farnham-Diggory (1992) has another suggestion. He explains that,

a large number of small abnormalities develop during prenatal life, each involving some irregularity in neurone arrangement, e.g. clumps of immature brain cells or congenital tumours. The growing brain compensates for these problems by rewiring around the problem area. These rewirings in turn may scramble normal information processing procedures just enough to make reading or calculation or any specific task very difficult.

Other researchers consider that some children with dyspraxia may have retained some primitive reflexes. These cause involuntary movements, e.g. shrugging, twitching, fidgeting. They prevent the development of more segmented movements. Blythe (1992) explains this. He claims that,

the continued presence of a cluster of aberrant reflexes causes writing and copying difficulties, impaired short term memory, the inability to sit still, excessive daydreaming, clumsiness and to a lesser degree mathematical problems.

and these are all observed difficulties in dyspraxia.

Another reported cause is in birth trauma. Cotrell (1992) examined 135 cases of 'learning disabled' – note not specifically dyspraxic children – and found that some form of birth difficulty had occurred. These he named as premature birth, precipitate birth, late delivery, forceps delivery, caesarean section, breech delivery, foetal anoxia and induced labour. And, of course, ongoing research, given that there are families where several members have dyspraxia or dyslexia or another possibly linked syndrome, is trying to identify genes so that in the future, prenatal intervention may be possible.

Like the condition, the answer to 'what is the cause?' is complex. Different researchers have made contributions from their own work which has been undertaken in different environments – schools, hospitals and laboratories – with different numbers of children being assessed in different ways. The children may have been observed doing different everyday coping skills at home or carrying out learning activities in the classroom. If observations are made on several occasions in different environments, e.g. the child in the playground to see if and how relationships with peers develop, or within the home considering how the child copes in the kitchen as distinct from the bedroom where skills of getting dressed are required, then the results are going to be quite different from those obtained by a paediatrician or occupational therapist who has restricted time with the child. On those occasions too, the child may be unnaturally tense in the presence of strangers – especially if he suspects he is going to fail some kind of test. And so, when reading about research, it is always useful to ask, 'How many children were assessed? What form did the assessment take? How long did the assessment last? What steps were taken to reduce bias in the collection of data?' (Macintyre 2000b)

Whatever the cause, 'the difficulties which confront children are troublesome and diverse' (Dobie 1996) – and it goes without saying that they must all be helped.

Labelling

The final discussion in this chapter concerns labelling and it is just as contentious as the issues that have gone before. Certainly a label such as dyspraxia allows parents and teachers to have a common basis for communication, for parents can be increasingly sure that the teachers will have a working knowledge of the condition. Let's list the points 'for labelling' first.

Labelling is helpful if it,

- gives an accurate indication of what is and what is not wrong,
- allows communication between parents, teachers and therapists,
- means getting help is easier with a specific label than without one,
- allows parents and children to belong to a support group and this reduces isolation,

- means that children can meet other children with dyspraxia who know how they feel,
- allows parents to share strategies and helpful ideas, even just let off steam,
- means shared ideas can give everyone confidence in trying new moves, and
- provides the possibility of a disability living allowance to help offset costs.

On the other hand:

- parents and the children themselves may not like the idea,
- there is not a definite cut off point – rather the condition is 'not being able to do certain things well' which is woolly and unhelpful for borderline children,
- the label may suggest an unchanging static picture of difficulties and this is not the case,
- the label suggests a global condition and yet only one or two areas may be problematic,
- as aspects of other conditions blend with dyspraxia, it may be possible to be given the wrong label!

NB Whether they are labelled or not, these children can be helped; the label need not stick (Caan 1998).

CHAPTER 3

Perceptual-motor development

The following chapter examines why some children cannot ride a bike or tie their laces. It studies the underlying abilities as well as offering advice which would be specific to teaching one particular skill. Despite Cowden and Eason's (1991) claim that 'movement problems may be more difficult to eliminate than other deficiency classifications', it should be stressed that short, regular spells of practice, especially when the children are cooperative and motivated, can make a huge difference. This is just as well, for if children are to be able to cope at home and at school, they must be able to carry out a wide range of activities. They must initiate some action plans and respond appropriately to others, sometimes very quickly. If they have a perceptual difficulty, for example if they take information from the environment incorrectly, they are miscued and the resulting actions are awkward or inappropriate. If there is no help, children can lose confidence and become fearful of moving at all. This leads to lack of practice which makes the problem worse. There is a further implication, however. French and Lee (1996) write:

> It is widely accepted that the development of controlled movement has a part to play in the intellectual development of children. Children need to experience movement in order to learn about themselves, the relationship to the environment and the interaction of the two.

This shows how important learning to move is. The implications of not moving well spread beyond the movement patterns or skills themselves into the children's intellectual, social and emotional development, particularly affecting their self-concept and self-esteem. This 'picture which children build of themselves' influences how they are able to form relationships with others, a critical part of social development. Knowing where they are in relation to outside objects and people out there in the environment allows them to orientate themselves in space so that they are not 'always bumping and getting bruised'. It also helps them judge where they are in relation to others – faulty judgments can cause them to intrude into other people's personal space and this can be very annoying – not a good way to make friends. This sense is kinaesthetic awareness which is the first sense to be explained under the heading 'perception'.

Perceptual information comes to the brain through the senses as shown in Figure 3.1.

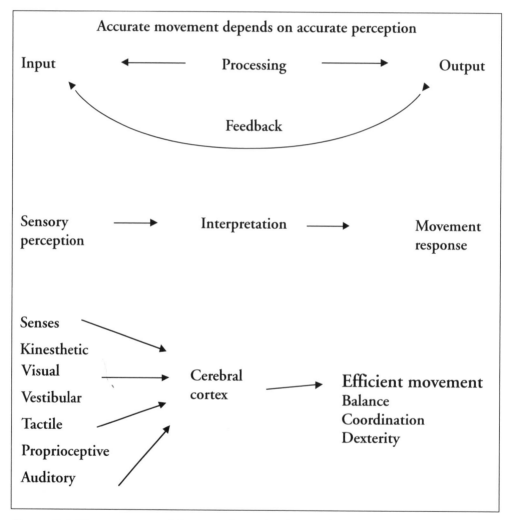

Figure 3.1 The senses and the part they play in moving well

If children, or adults for that matter, are to move efficiently and effectively, achieving the purpose of the action without extraneous movement, they have to appreciate how their bodies are functioning in the space around them. They have to realise how near they are to other people and objects and the distance between themselves and different things out there in the environment (this is spatial awareness). They have to know where their different body parts are in relation to each other and realise the effect moving one part has on the others (this is body awareness). They also need to know where their bodies end and the outside world begins (this is called body boundary). (Figure 3.2)

Figure 3.2 Kinesthetic awareness

The words (concepts) children need to understand if their spatial awareness is poorly developed are:

- near
- above
- along
- beyond
- forward
- far away
- below
- through
- beside
- backwards
- sideways (this last one is very difficult – children may not develop a true awareness of laterality before nine years+)

and familiarisation can happen in the classroom and the hall, even in the playground when the weather is fine. In the school hall, all sorts of apparatus layouts can help spatial orientation, especially if teachers remember to stress the spatial concepts as the children enjoy the movement. Perhaps the younger children can say the words 'through, under, over', as they go and the older ones can try to remember their route and draw it out (mapping skills) when they go back to the class. This also stimulates the short term memory, which is a major problem for children with dyspraxia. If the children work in groups, the ones with difficulties won't feel so exposed and even if the others do most of the remembering, it doesn't matter, because they are actually helping the dyspraxic children to recall what went on some time ago in a different setting.

In the classroom, all sorts of 2-D activities such as 'join the dots' with explanations such as 'these dots are near each other so you just need a little line and some are far away so your pencil has to travel a long way', help the younger ones appreciate short distances. For the older children 'Lost in the maze' puzzles with questions such as, 'How is the policeman going to catch the convict?' should elicit replies such as, 'Well, he'll have to go forward a short way, then up over the bridge and through the wood. That's a long way'. These simple activities promote awareness of distance, help the children internalise the spatial concepts and also, and very importantly, help planning and organisation. The children have to make decisions about where to go and also think about the order or sequence of events, i.e. do this and then that. If they trace the route with their pencil, then their fine motor control is being practised too. More complex questions can challenge older children, e.g. 'Where will the convict go to escape?' This route would be likely to take the convict backwards into the maze and this needs a much more sophisticated appreciation of the problem.

Perhaps after trying some of the activities above, one group of children could set up a maze with gym apparatus in the hall or design a treasure map for another group to follow. All activities which help them to appreciate 'where to go' can be lots of fun for all the children. The important thing is that parents and teachers recognise the important learning possibilities within simple, everyday games. Hugely complex ideas are not required. An analysis of some old-fashioned favourites to identify the learning possibilities does very well. Even pinning the tail on the donkey (using Blu Tack), involves fine motor skills and spatial awareness – judging distances in a fun way. Who remembers 'In and out the dusky bluebells'? The party game is old-fashioned, but the idea of a circle of children making arches for some to weave their way 'under and through, moving from back to front' certainly could be adapted to produce a similar game which would help develop spatial concepts as well as laterality – awareness of movement at the sides.

Dressing the clown – or the cowboy or other characters for the school assembly – can be an appropriate activity, for this can also help with the organisation of getting dressed at home which is difficult for some dyspraxic children. Children of different ages can have fun with this activity. The teacher or the older children produce a simple outline of the character and then the younger ones have to dress him. This can be with actual clothes shapes which they have drawn, or if recognition of shapes (triangles, rectangles, circles, hexagons, etc.) is an appropriate learning focus at this time, the children can stick on circles for buttons, make a bow tie out of triangles, use rectangles for shoes and so on. Again it is helpful if adults can control the pace of the activity so that its purpose is not lost, e.g. 'What

Clown

will we put on first? What do we need next?' The actual sticking the shapes on to the body helps fine motor control.

All sorts of variations of this can be used, e.g. drawing round the children themselves to make life-size models and then dressing them up for a disco or going to a wedding – whatever! This simple to prepare kind of activity can be enjoyed by all of the children in the class; it's not expensive and inherently it houses so many learning skills to do with spatial awareness and body awareness, i.e. the other aspect of kinesthetic awareness. After the 'models' are complete, the children can explain why they are dressed this way and even use them as a stimulus for a play. Sometimes the children get too enthusiastic and the models get cluttered, so simplicity is the name of the game!

Once the children grasp the concept of distance, they can have fun working on, 'How near?', or 'How far?', i.e. challenges which involve estimating distances.

How many big steps forwards will you need to reach Ian? Four? Let's try!

Stories or songs with kites, e.g. 'Let's go fly a kite' from Mary Poppins, then making kites and later trying to fly them, houses lots of possibilities for science and craft and shape awareness and appreciation of the spatial concept, 'above'. This is often a difficult one for many children to grasp, even for those who do not have dyspraxia.

When people mention 'distances' they usually think of quite long ways apart. But children writing stories, as they do at all stages of the primary school, constantly have to judge distances between one word and the next. 'Keep your words spaced out', is the instruction on many jotters. The children are sometimes urged to measure the space with their finger but this requires crossing the midline, a task which dyspraxic children find extremely difficult. If sequencing is difficult, the written page can appear as a jumble of letters, yet the dyspraxic children are clear about what they want to say. Opportunities for oral reporting or using a computer are often the best ways to try to help as the amalgam of difficulties outlined above interact to prevent 'good writing'. (Figure 3.3)

Figure 3.3 Examples of children's writing

Handwriting practice is a very worrying time for children with dyspraxia. Before they begin they know they are not as good as others in the class. Their letter formation is invariably poor and can be in the wrong order due to poor auditory sequencing. Furthermore, the children anticipating a poor result are likely to be tense. 'My brain knows what my hands are to do', explains Grace, 'but they just won't do it. And I can't do it again, because when my hands are tired, it's even worse.'

Repetition is not the answer, for it usually means more failure. Allowing Grace to use the computer and praising her work for the language content or the imaginative ideas is much kinder than worrying her with presentation issues – after all she won't have to write by hand very often in later life. The actual scribing is a less important skill than the ones she can probably do, but if it has to be endured,

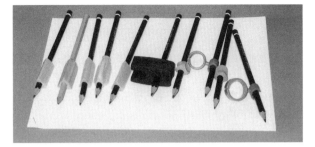

A selection of pencil grips

then making sure the child is well supported on a suitable chair so that she doesn't feel insecure, helping her with the angle of her paper, especially if she is left-handed, and making sure she has enough time in a quiet place are all helpful strategies.

If children have to write a story, then drawing pictures illustrating the sequence of events gives a visual reminder and often lets children continue without constant help. This both relieves the teacher and lets the child feel independent. It also stops other children becoming resentful about the extra support the dyspraxic ones usually require.

Body awareness

It really is quite amazing how much children and adults take for granted. Doing up buttons without looking; tying a bow behind one's back; playing an accordion where the two hands cope with vastly different jobs; folding arms – the intricate uses of the different body parts are endless. But moving them in a coordinated way depends on an accurate sense of where they are in relation to one another and being able to cope when the movement of one part affects the others.

Proprioceptors

— any receptor that supplys info about state of the body – muscles etc.

Many children, especially those with dyspraxia, lack the sense of placement which proprioceptors should provide. If they want to step up onto a chair, for example, they will look to check where the supporting foot is in relation to the chair – they won't be able to sense its position. This is because their proprioceptors, or nerve endings in the muscles and skin, are not relaying information as they should. Lots of actions are affected. Sitting down without looking involves a judgment of where the body is in relation to the chair and this in turn tells how much strength or release of strength is required to carry out the movement efficiently. A child lifting a cup needs to know where and when to curl his fingers round the handle and how much strength to use so that the liquid does not spill. Those with efficient proprioceptors will manage this easily, almost automatically, but children with difficulty will clutch the cup against themselves for extra support and have to look closely every step of the way.

Graeme's spatial orientation (1)   Graeme's spatial orientation (2)

This little boy was not able to pull his leg back into the hoops so that he could continue. He had to readjust his body so that he could look back through his arms to his feet. Without looking he had no sense of where his feet were! Games like Blind Man's Buff or any other activity where visual cues are cut out is impossible for this child, because that would mean that two senses, i.e. visual and auditory, were not able to help his spatial orientation.

Body boundary

If children are sitting together on the carpet in class, those with poor proprioceptive feedback will not keep a space between themselves and the other children. They don't realise they are crowding and bumping till it happens and they are scolded by the teacher or the other children push them away. Even more important is the fact that a poor sense of body boundary can affect safety. Children don't realise how close they are to the edge of the kerb or the edge of the swimming pool. Parents and teachers have to constantly watch out for everyday tasks which herald danger for these children. This can be time consuming and wearing for the adults and equally frustrating for the children when they reach the stage of wanting to be independent.

Tactile

This is a most interesting sense and difficulties are perhaps less well understood than in the more obvious ones. There are two aspects to consider. Firstly, some children can't bear to be touched. Even brushing lightly against them can cause them to overreact, sometimes lashing out – to the dismay and surprise of the offending adult or child. Sometimes they can't endure taking hands in a circle, and the other children naturally feel rejected as they don't understand the source of the refusal and take it personally. This same over-sensitivity can cause ructions at hair cutting or nail clipping times as the sensations are felt much more severely than normal. Some children cry with the hurt of it all. Wearing a watch can only be tolerated if the strap is smooth and made of leather – not plastic as it is more likely to stick to the skin. Some children wear their socks inside out as the seams irritate them all day. This extreme sensitivity can be seen as allergies in some children.

The second touch difficulty comes when children need hard feedback from the environment. The children are asking their proprioceptors to do their job and send them messages which let them orientate themselves in space. These are the children who thump around. Everyone says, 'They don't know their own strength'. The child who is constantly out sharpening his pencil is one – because when he pressed too hard the lead broke! The teacher may see this as an avoidance tactic and be cross. Maybe a harder lead pencil or a ball pen could be the answer? Combine this 'too fast and too strong' approach with distance misjudgments, and you can understand why teachers don't give dyspraxic children responsible jobs which most children love to have. And of course the child who bumps and clatters can irritate other children too and when toys are broken or precious things are spoiled, patience does run out!

And so, although taking hands in a circle or in a line may sound a simple instruction, to a dyspraxic child, it can hold miseries best avoided and repercussions which are extremely hurtful, especially when they are not understood.

Vision and hearing

The most obvious benefit of vision is to be able to see clearly and recognise people and objects and the distance between them, while hearing is an important listening and learning mode, one which drives communication. Dyspraxic children may not have seeing or hearing problems per se – or at least not more than other children – however their functional vision and hearing may be problematic. What does this mean for the affected children?

Distractibility

Auditory
Most children learn to cut out background movements and/or any extraneous noise and this allows them to focus in and concentrate on the teaching at school or

on instructions at home. Children with dyspraxia however can't do this. They hear all the background noises. They have sensitive hearing and pick up far too many signals. One little girl, distressed in an open plan school, explained, 'I can't hear the teacher for the noise!' When the mum arrived in high dudgeon to sort things out, she was amazed at the quiet atmosphere which was obviously not the exception, but the rule. And yet the child, now sitting close to the teacher, insisted she could not hear. No classroom has absolutely no noise, so the children who cannot cut out distractors are constantly beset by 'having to listen hard' all the time. Theatre visits too can be spoiled because the children can't make out the dialogue if there is any music or rustling of sweets.

Visual

In similar vein, children can be readily distracted by the least movement which falls into their field of vision. Leaves fluttering outside catch their eye and concentration is lost. Even the movement of another child's pencil can be distracting and yet, when social isolation is also a problem for most dyspraxic children, the idea of moving them to sit alone is not one which appeals.

Other visual difficulties

Tracking

A difficulty coming from the visual sense is tracking. This can mean that some children don't see an oncoming ball until it is too late to adjust the hands to grasp it and so they may swerve to avoid it altogether; some children won't be able to follow the path of a paper aeroplane or follow a skier coming down a slope. Much more importantly and dangerously, some won't be able to judge the oncoming approach of a car or bus in terms of distance or speed. Link this with impulsiveness and it is easy to see why children need constant supervision if they are to stay safe. Being a parent of a dyspraxic child is a full time occupation.

Tracking of course affects copying from the board. By the time the child has found the correct place on the board and then looked down to a jotter, the place on the board has been lost. Having an inclined desk board can make a big difference, because the transition from vertical to horizontal is reduced.

The vital message from parents, however, is 'cut down the amount of work the children have to do!' Some parents copy all the sums out in jotters for their children and leave the children to fill in the answers. Could classroom assistants do this for children whose parents can't or won't carry out this task? Parents report that reducing the workload in this kind of way has made a tremendous difference because their children can now keep up with the rest of their group. Imagine the positive input to these children's self-esteem. To know you are not going to be last is such a huge relief.

Example

Nadia explained, 'I was always afraid of being last. I dreaded hearing, "Come on Nadia, last again, we haven't got all day, you know." It got to the stage that I spent so much time trying to find out where other people were on the page, that I got even further behind. To make matters worse, they thought I was copying! However, now I don't have so many sums to do. I can do the actual sums anyway, I just can't do them fast when there's lots of writing.'

Tracking is also important in reading and mathematics. If the letters on the page wobble or if poor sequencing causes the eyes to jump over letters, then pages of small text are extremely daunting. It is easy to blow up text on a photocopier which may help. Another job for a classroom assistant? This difficulty also affects being able to write in a straight line – perhaps tilting the paper in line with the writer could help. Similarly in mathematics, children find it difficult to line up columns of figures and if these are written incorrectly then the answer will always be wrong. This despite the actual arithmetical function being correct. The only way forward is for teachers to have the time and opportunity to effect an accurate diagnosis of where the child's difficulties lie. If this doesn't happen the teacher will think the child doesn't understand and try to change the teaching method whereas it's not comprehension but spatial planning that is causing the problem. Accurate assessment is the key. This takes skill and practice, but it is essential if dyspraxic children are to flourish.

Three dimensional vision
Another visual difficulty is often in poor three dimensional vision. If children see objects as flat against the background rather then standing out from it, it is not difficult to understand why bumping and bruising occurs . . . the table is seen as being slightly further away than it really is and approaching it means bumped legs and juice being spilt or clattered down, and in the cloakroom coats don't fix on pegs because the hanging action misses the target! In the classroom, the children with poor perception of depth may not be able to interpret visual aids and they certainly won't appreciate perspective in art classes. Some children can't find their shoes if they lie on a patterned carpet. So both at school and at home plain backgrounds can save time and effort in focusing through complex patterns or hunting for things that are not really lost.

This visual perception problem of misjudging distance can work against children making friends too. Some cannot bear their personal space to be invaded; they are extremely protective of that space. If they have faulty perception of distance, whenever another child comes too near they freak out, or alternatively shy away creating a new space for themselves. The approaching child who had no intention of imposing usually doesn't wait to find out what is wrong and a chance of making a friend is lost.

Auditory difficulties

Children who listen well have a good chance of learning well. If hearing is a problem, responses to instructions can be delayed and this causes problems from rising till bedtime. If the children have to concentrate hard to hear clearly – all day long – they just have to have a break and so 'switch off'. When adults say, 'He's in a world of his own', this is what they mean. The other world is far too busy. Understanding this, teachers can organise short spells of activity and very quiet times. Some schools have a quiet room which children from different classes can use. This is wonderful for dyspraxic children and it gives everyone a break.

Vestibular

Vestibular receptors are situated in the inner ear and work to coordinate movements which require balance. This is why children with an ear infection can find they feel off balance; this can even cause them to feel very sick. Children without balance difficulties will not be so severely affected. In fact they may actually search out this sensation of vertigo by visiting the fairground. There the whirling and spinning causes them to lose and regain balance. Others hate this feeling of being out of control.

   In dyspraxia, the vestibular and proprioceptor senses may not give enough feedback for the children to have an accurate picture of where they are in relation to objects in their environment or how the body parts relate to one another and this can result in the lurching gait and clumsy movements which many such children have. The vestibular sense should initiate responses to changes in the head position, automatically coordinating the head and body.

How to help

Lots of games appropriately structured to the children's specific profile of difficulties are the answer. Why do these need to be known? Well, teachers in the gym might prepare an activity where two children standing closely back to back have to lean against each other to lower into a sitting position. The activity could help children with poor body awareness feel where their backs are, through the pressure exerted by the other child. This could be very useful unless the dyspraxic child was one who could not bear to be touched – one who was extremely sensitive. Then the choice of activity would be very wrong for that child, causing him to be really upset if not harmed. The teachers across the curriculum must be clear about each child's profile and be careful not to intervene unwisely.

There are lots of songs and rhymes for the younger children which do not have this contact problem, e.g. 'Hands, shoulders, knees and toes', 'Incy wincy spider', 'Simon says', to name but a few (for other suggestions, see Chapter 8).

Types of movement and movement abilities

All of the senses which have been described should work together to help produce movement which is appropriate, i.e. which is in the right direction, using the correct amount of strength and speed. Other words which describe efficient movement would be:

rhythmic, coordinated and balanced.

These describe the movement abilities which underlie all competent movement patterns, no matter whether they are:

1. gross movements,
2. fine movements, or
3. manipulative skills.

Gross movements

Gross movements use the large muscle groups which work together to produce actions such as walking, running, jumping and climbing. They need a good deal of strength, control which comes from the body being balanced and whole body coordination. These basic movement patterns develop as children mature, although children with dyspraxia will tend to develop them at the later end of the 'normal' time range and will be seen to use more effort than children without this difficulty. While most, but certainly not all dyspraxic children, are rather ungainly, they do achieve the everyday patterns at a level which allows them to carry out routine tasks and coping skills at an acceptable level of competence.

Fine movements

The demands made by fine movements are different – speaking, eating, writing and playing the piano are examples that show that only small body parts are used. This can be easier for some children, because when one part of the body is 'fixed', as in sitting, it does not need to be controlled and full concentration can go to the moving parts. But of course fine movements can be very intricate, involving hand – eye coordination, – e.g. cutting food and threading beads, or greater rhythmical awareness, e.g. in playing

Playing the piano

the piano, or significant control in a small area, e.g. in writing or colouring in. Playing the piano is a very useful activity because the sound indicates the strength that is being used; short, easy tunes are motivating and hands can be watched as they gain control and, through that, fluency.

These movements also can involve the children in 'crossing the midline of the body' as in drawing a rainbow or reaching across to tie laces on the other foot and this is very often tricky. In fact, finding that children have this difficulty can be one of the key indicators of dyspraxia. Teachers need to note this difficulty carefully in any profile of needs. A related difficulty comes if children have not established hand dominance. This may not happen till children are six years old, but it can cause the children to appear uncoordinated and clumsy when they fumble because they are undecided in which hand to use.

Manipulative skills

This kind of activity requires that the children cope with outside objects such as pencils or bats, knives and forks. To do this they have to cope with added control demands, e.g. holding the swinging bat against the impact of the ball. They also have to have a developed sense of body boundary – where they end and the object begins. And of course they have to make the object follow a pattern when writing or a trajectory when throwing a ball. This takes practice and can be very difficult if muscle tone is poor. Children with poor shoulder control will find it difficult to control a pencil, especially if they are not sitting at the correct height of table. Having a triangular grip can help children whose pincer grip is not well developed or retained. Retained palmer reflexes mean that the hand will curl round the pencil and this results in an awkward grip which makes writing very difficult for the child and illegible for the reader. But readers have to persevere because wonderful stories can be hidden in a messy text.

Timing of development

In young children, gross movements involving balance and coordination of the large muscle groups are generally developed first. This explains why some children can run yet be unable to control a pencil. And of course children have been practising these kinds of movements longer! This sequence of development also explains why children's difficulties may not be apparent in the earliest stages. Parents can miss fine motor skill difficulties because they assume that because the gross motor skills are achieved, the others, that is the fine motor skills, will be proficient as well. Some children, however, can carry out fine motor skills well and yet not manage the gross movements in a coordinated way at all. It would be interesting to know what part practice plays in this. For if children fall and get hurt, as they try to run and jump, they are likely to avoid the scenario which caused the pain and so they may prefer to have jigsaws or art work. Practice then brings success and this gives the child positive reinforcement and motivation to continue.

Assessing movement patterns

Every movement, large or small, has three parts. (Figure 3.4)

Figure 3.4 Analysis of a movement pattern

When movement is smooth and efficient, the three parts flow together and the momentum from one part carries on to help the next. In sequential movements, the recovery from the first completed movement blends with the preparation for the second. Flowing movement has an inbuilt rhythm and an awareness of this can clarify the pattern, for example where the strong parts need to come, and so help the pattern to be done well. Children can be helped to 'listen' for the rhythm, then clap or stamp it out. This is very good for children who have difficulty listening, for it helps them visualise a successful movement pattern.

In efficient movement, the preparatory phase 'gets the body ready' by deciding on the speed that will be needed, the direction of travel, the parts of the body to be used and the sequence of the action. Complex movement patterns require a great deal of mental planning and preparation. Think of attempting a long jump or even the triple jump. All of the stride pattern and timing elements have to be rehearsed before the athletes begin! This is why they take some time contemplating all the demands of the task before setting off. Children attempting tasks such as running and jumping off a bench, challenges which can be just as demanding for them, may have the added difficulty of watching others to ensure that they will not run across their path and spoil their attempt. Children who can't plan ahead, who can't visualise what comes next, have to make on-the-spot decisions and if they are flustered by being rushed they may well make the wrong ones. Similarly, children who can't cut out visual distractors have difficulties because other children running by cause them to lose their concentration. Lots of children need more time, more help and possibly less challenge if they are to stay safe.

Balance

The most crucial movement ability is balance. It is central to all movement – much more than being able to stand still or adjusting the body weight to allow standing on one leg. This is static balance or postural control and it is important in maintaining poise and posture, but there is also dynamic balance which controls the body as it moves, working perhaps to sustain equilibrium in a jump or in a forward roll or when the body changes direction. If adults wish to assess children's balance, they must observe the child moving and being still.

Children with dyspraxia can find balance difficult and they often have to be helped to adopt positions which help their postural control, e.g. by being supported by a classroom wall when others are sitting without support; by having a frame or handle near the toilet so that they may sit securely; by having their feet supported if their desk is too high for them to have a secure writing position. This is very important, for if the children have to struggle to maintain their balance, they have less energy to concentrate on whatever else needs to be learned.

Vision helps considerably in maintaining balance, and if the dyspraxic child's functional vision isn't good, giving him a point in space to 'fix' his attention on can help. Then he can align his body position with that spot. Mirrors only provide back-to-front cues and can be confusing, although some children are helped by seeing themselves. Often it's a case of trying different strategies out in a fun, non-threatening way.

Steering a bike

Balancing and learning to ride a bike

Nearly all children want to learn to ride a bike. It's a symbol of growing up as well as the means to travel further afield with friends. Dyspraxic children find this very difficult because of the balance, coordination and steering demands and because their cues from the environment may cause them to make faulty judgments about the edge of the safe path. Many teachers would say 'leave teaching this skill till the child's movement abilities have improved', – the trouble being that the children won't wait, they desperately want to ride the bike now!

What advice could be offered to help?

First the bike has to be small enough so that the child can place two feet firmly on the ground and the frame has to be sturdy enough to give real support. If not, the control demands may be too great. Then the child should sit astride the bike and propel himself along a flat, even path for grass tends to be too bumpy or sticky. Once the child is confident that he can keep the bike upright, then move to a gentle slope which flattens out and do the same again. Do not try to put the feet on the pedals – rather lift the legs a little way keeping them ready to stop.

Only when this has been achieved should the child worry about the pedals, for if he tries to use the pedals too soon, the problem of not being able to judge the correct amount of strength means that too much may be applied and the bike will probably tip over or take off at speed. This gives the child a fright and his confidence will take a knock even if his body doesn't! Some children will need to look down to see where their feet are before they can place them on the pedals so adults should offer some physical support them at this point. Still keep on a gentle slope because this will provide just enough momentum. There should be enough distance for the bike to travel in a straight line so that there are no steering problems at this stage.

Steering can be difficult. There are so many other things to think about that many children go round in circles. This happens when they lean too heavily on the handlebars so check that the seat is comfortable and at the correct height. Sometimes drawing a circle on paper and explaining what happens if the handle bars are turned too sharply, can help children who learn best through visual cues. Above all, remember how difficult learning to drive was and stay calm as you persevere, for when the child manages, it will be a real cause for celebration and the sense of achievement will do lots to cement a happy relationship.

Kerr turning too shaprly

Speed of movement

This refers to the time taken to react to a stimulus and to move at a chosen and appropriate speed. Understanding the difference between the two can help clarify a child's difficulties and therefore contribute to accurate assessment.

Stimulus presented	Response initiated	Response completed
Reaction time	Movement time	

Figure 3.5 Analysing movements in terms of speed.

Reaction time
(i)   Reaction Time is the term used to describe the time between the perception of a given stimulus and the beginning of the response. Children with quick reaction time tend to do well in competitive activities of short duration, e.g. sprinting, net play in badminton, or in games where instructions are called out and the pupils are required to make an immediate response.
NB Reaction time should not to be confused with reflex action, which is purely automatic.
(ii)   Movement Time is the time the action takes from beginning to completion.
(iii)   Response Time (RT + MT) covers both reaction and movement time.

In analysing a poorly carried out action, it is important to keep the two 'times' in mind, for poor performance in one does not necessarily indicate poor performance in the other. Reaction time can be improved by focusing the child's attention firmly on the stimulus and perhaps giving prior warning of any sudden response, e.g. fixing eye contact with the child as you say 'Are you ready' at the start of a race. Improving the movement time requires analysis of the movement pattern into its preparatory, action and recovery stages, so that appropriate correction may be made as necessary.

   To summarise these details, a movement observation checklist is given in Appendix 1. This is to facilitate recording while observing the children as they practise and become ever more effective and efficient movers and hopefully more confident youngsters. For children who are consistently clumsy of functioning at a level below that of their peers, specific tests to measure their ability in balance, co-ordination, speed of movement, body awareness, spatial and rhythmic awareness, may be needed. These tests, which are fun to do, have been specifically designed to isolate the faulty component so that effective remediation can then be planned.

However it must be said that test results usually hold no surprises for teachers who have had the opportunity to study their children over time and in different environments. Tests don't claim to do more than measure performance on more than one occasion, and assessors, despite trying to put children at their ease, recognise the stress factors (new venue, 'testers', not knowing the implications of the outcome), which are sure to bias the results.

CHAPTER 4

Intellectual development in the dyspraxic child

Many children with dyspraxia have average or above average intelligence when measured on an IQ test and so a chapter on intellectual development may seem superfluous. But just as the optician who says the child can 'see perfectly well' and the audiologist who reports 'no problem with hearing', those who wish to understand their children's difficulties – and given their level of intelligence, these can be surprising – must consider the children's functional intelligence, because here, as in all the other aspects of development, perceptual miscues impair performance. This understanding needs to underpin any assessment of the child's 'ability to do'. When talking about children with dyspraxia, it might be useful to consider a more functional description of intelligence, e.g. 'the ability to react appropriately in any given situation'.

Assessing the dyspraxic child in this way can give a different picture. However, if assessments are not to be distorted, they must be made over a range of activities when the child is not tired or has been concentrating too long or is in a new environment, because then the strangeness of the surroundings could affect the child's response. My plea to everyone is to differentiate between these different definitions of intelligence and gear the child's learning to the one which needs most help. In practical terms what does this mean?

- If the child can do it (and it is always best to check this orally), then give the child fewer sums, less writing, less reading, little homework, i.e. remove any unnecessary 'motor' burden.
- Help the child with organisational tasks by keeping to a known routine and breaking down instructions into manageable chunks, i.e. reduce any planning burden.
- Don't confuse inability to do these planning and organising jobs with the inability to do academic tasks.

How can we help children with dyspraxia to learn in school? They will have poor short term memories and short attention spans. Because of this they need instructions repeated over and over again or some other form of aide-memoire has to be devised. They will be easily distracted from the task at hand and if their hands won't do what their brain tells them to do, they will be frustrated and angry and may resort to all kinds of inappropriate behaviour. But they are bright and while this causes them to recognise their limitations (but not really understand them, because after all they have always been like this and know no other way), it may mean that they need to complete fewer examples of things they can do well. This allows them to get a page finished and keep up with their friends. This does mean that the teacher and classroom assistant have extra preparation and when there are 32 others this is difficult, but there will be an enormous payback in having a more relaxed, responsive child. And if there is co-morbidity, i.e. if children with other syndromes have some of the same difficulties, then perhaps the plans will be suitable for these children too. It is best if these can be applied quite subtly however, as children with difficulties will not necessarily relish being put together in the same group. This could lay them open to taunting, although this depends of course on the ethos of the school and how the children have responded to being taught to respect one another. We have to recognise that 'the stupid table' still exists in the minds of some children. It is best to be forewarned about possible consequences of seating arrangements, even though they may never happen.

Let's consider some of the underlying competences which children need to help them to learn.

Concentrating

Being able to concentrate influences what children learn and how much they can learn in one spell. Many children can concentrate for an inordinate amount of time – even in the nursery some children ask for longer to spend on their craft work, perhaps making jewellery or construction work or building roads and rivers in the sand. Interestingly, this ability seems to be pervasive across different activities – it's the same children who can concentrate like this, no matter what they are asked to do. This means the ability is in the child rather than being dependent on the activity. If this is so, these children must be able to focus and find interesting things in a range of activities. Perhaps with dyspraxic children teachers could usefully point out these interesting features because the children's lack of concentration may have caused them to overlook them. It is understandable to assume that these children appreciate what is self-evident to the others, but this is not always the case.

Children who can concentrate like this usually win the approval of the teacher because concentration means success and this provides good feedback and endorses the planning and preparation that have gone before. Children who find it difficult to concentrate however, tend to flit from one task to another, never finishing anything which satisfies them or their teacher. Their attention span is brief and they are impulsive, so they go off without any thought for the consequences. But why should this be?

Wood (1992) found that many young children just have not developed the capacity for retaining involvement and he surmised that this was due to their lack of organisational ability – the children could neither organise the materials they required for successful completion of the task nor visualise the end product. If this is so, it certainly explains why tasks are abandoned. The best kind of help could be discussing the planning and resources and helping the children decide on the sequence of events which will enable them to complete their task. Asking the children to sit and concentrate is self-defeating, if the underlying planning and organising abilities are not there.

Dyspraxic children definitely need to be shown how to organise and plan their work, and if the activity lasts for some time, this needs to be repeated over and over again. There is a subtle but important distinction between helping children complete the end product, be it a painting, a model or a puzzle, and helping them with the process – the organisation. This sounds as if it is particularly relevant for children with dyspraxia, as helping children plan what they wish to do rather than helping them complete the end product matches these children's needs. Teachers must distinguish between planning/organisational difficulties and conceptual/understanding difficulties if their help is to be appropriate. In story writing, for example, children will be frustrated to be given 'more words' to make their story more imaginative, if sequencing is the real problem.

Memorising

A second ability is memorising, with or without really understanding the meaning of the task, e.g. rote learning times tables or using jingles as an aide–memoire. Very often the jingle is remembered long after the learning it was to ease! One early years maths intervention programme (2000) asks children to memorise numbers up to 100 in a rhythmical, jingle kind of way. Certainly the children are enthusiastic and appear pleased by their success. The instigators of this approach claim that the 'understanding' of what the numbers mean will come later and more easily if sequences of numbers can be readily recalled. The scheme is in its infancy. It will be interesting to see if this method of promoting technical mastery then understanding, rather than the two together, works. Could this help dyspraxic children who have short term memory problems?

Helping memorising

Example

One mum, Sarah, told me that she had a tape of times tables with music. This had lots of repetition of tables at different speeds and whenever she was with her daughter (who was dyspraxic) in the car, she played the tape. Sometimes they repeated the jingles together, other times the tape just played with her little girl seemingly paying little heed. But the regularity and the repetition paid off, at least at the level of instant recall, and the little girl was so pleased to be able to answer quickly and correctly in class. Sarah explained, 'We had to keep at it and at it. Some days she seemed to have forgotten lots of answers she knew before. It wasn't easy and sometimes it was difficult for both of us not to show our frustration. However we devised a "whoops" game and when answers didn't come readily we'd say "whoops!" This sounds strange, but it took the pressure off and made us smile. I knew if I got cross, that would be the end of the practising, so "whoops" was a strategy to keep the routine going.'

Children with dyspraxia often have difficulty remembering what went before, such as the content of previous lessons, and so it is very useful to have 'advance organisers' or recaps, be it pictures or tapes or videos to prod the memories of children with these difficulties before the new lesson begins.

Transfer of learning

The ability to memorise appears to develop as the children mature. Researchers who set out to understand how young children memorise, showed them a number of objects, covered them, then asked the children to remember as many as they could. The children made a random and very short list. The researchers then showed the children how grouping the objects into categories of soft toys, pieces of fruit, could help them remember more things, and the children had several tries using this strategy. A little later however, these same children, despite having been more successful when they tried grouping, did not adopt this strategy again. The younger children immediately started calling out objects they could recall with no thought as to any 'method'. There was a developmental difference – the older children would recall the grouping strategy when reminded, but only after a time of guessing and being asked if they had not heard of a better way! Similarly with suggesting that memorising could be eased by rehearsal: repeating the names or numbers over and over as most adults do when trying to commit phone numbers or birthdays or shopping lists to memory. Even when the children found this successful on one occasion there was no guarantee that they would remember it or try it again. Maybe this reinforces the point that very young children need time to mature and develop different learning strategies and that 'forcing the pace' if this could be done, is unproductive. However, there are simple memory games like Kim's game which children enjoy, and they can try out the effectiveness of grouping objects themselves and judge whether indeed this is a good way for them to recall more items.

Problem-solving strategies

Another 'special skill' is building a range of problem-solving strategies so that when a problem is encountered, children can select the most appropriate and effective way of solving it. Flavell (1985) called this process of making children aware of the different strategies possible, metacognition, or in other words, making them aware of how they were learning. This sounds very helpful – if children are made aware of what they do and what they could do, surely they will use the more successful way? The snag is that alerting the children to a successful problem-solving strategy is a far cry from getting them to recall it and select it when a similar problem arises. This is why transfer of learning from one situation to another doesn't readily occur, even although it is difficult to understand why not.

It is also worth remembering that different children learn best in different ways. Lots of listening activities will suit some children and defeat those who learn best by seeing. Other children like to have 'hands-on' experiences and interactive activities help them retain the key learning points. Many dyspraxic children with tactile problems, however, will not be happy to have 'feely bag' activities because of the sensitivity in their hands. Some simply cannot bear rough materials, and not knowing what is in the bag. Some children will simply refuse to take part.

As teachers, we can be guilty of preparing learning materials to suit our own preferred way of learning because this is what comes naturally. To help dyspraxic children, however, we must identify their favoured way instead and construct learning materials based on these modes.

Different forms of intelligence

The idea that there are different preferred ways of learning fits well with the theory that there are different forms of intelligence. Gardner named six! These he called 'frames of mind'. These were:

- *linguistic intelligence*
  seen in those who use language fluently, or in a novel and appropriate way; in those who explain clearly or argue convincingly; in those who use language in an original, descriptive mode, such as poetry.
- *musical intelligence*
  seen in those who are particularly sensitive to rhythm and pitch. This is often expressed in the ability to sing well or play an instrument but may be housed in those who appreciate music in an analytic, considered way.
- *logical-mathematical intelligence*
  seen in those who remember facts, score well on tests which demand quick recall; in those who can apply known facts to new situations, i.e. transfer learning appropriately; in those who have organisational/planning skills. Mathematicians and scientists have this kind of intelligence.
- *spatial intelligence*
  seen in those who can visualise complex designs from different perspectives such as architects or graphic artists; those who can appreciate spatial moves, e.g. on a chess board, snooker table or sports field.
- *bodily kinesthetic intelligence*
  seen in those with accurate visual and kinesthetic perception; in those who require to balance precariously such as ballet dancers or tree surgeons; in those who use non-verbal behaviour to convey messages, e.g. mime artists or impressionists.
- *personal intelligence*
  seen in those who can interpret their own feelings accurately, and those who can interpret the feelings, moods, temperaments of others.

This last mode overlaps with Sternberg's contextual intelligence (1985). He develops Gardner's idea by talking of those who use their perception of others to manipulate their social setting. They tune in and then make the most of the situation: the child who consciously behaves in a way which will gain him praise or some other kind of reward. Often people talk of 'street wise children'. They are demonstrating contextual intelligence!

Gardner's (1983) 'frames of mind' complement the division of development into its social and emotional, perceptual-motor and intellectual aspects. In putting forward this differentiation, Gardner is supporting the curricular plan which from age three, advocates a wide experience of learning activities so that each mode of intelligence may have the opportunity to flourish.

The kinds of intelligence which dyspraxic children are least likely to display are the last two: bodily kinesthetic intelligence or body awareness which gives a precise picture of the position of the body in space and therefore contributes to efficient movement, and personal intelligence, because dyspraxic children find it difficult to view life from another person's perspective and this makes empathising with others problematic. This will be discussed in detail in the chapter on social development. Parents, however, can be comforted by the fact that there are these different forms. Because of that differentiation, all children will find learning in some ways easier than others. If children have difficulties in one area, then it may be that other, perhaps less obvious talents, such as the ability to play a musical instrument, are there.

Intelligence Quotient

IQ tests were originally designed to have only items which were culture and experience free so that they could claim to measure innate potential without any environmental effect. They tried to measure the range of skills which indicated likely success in schools 'and they do this quite well for a limited number of topics' (Bee 1995). What they don't do, is cover competences like creative or original thinking, the ability to find a novel solution to a problem, or social skills, e.g. the ability to adjust to fit into a group, or movement skills, e.g. the ability to adjust one's movement to suit a changing terrain, all aspects covered by Gardner in his 'frames of mind' model of intelligence.

As a result, an IQ test is a very specific tool, useful to identify differences in children at any one time, but its limitations must be recognised, for even the stress of having a test could surely alter the score. This of course could be exacerbated by parents. If they see the test as a measure which will determine their child's success in life, they may well pass on anxieties about 'doing well' to their children, and unwittingly cause them to 'freeze'. Some may buy test books and attempt to teach the test. Perhaps this explains why many authorities no longer use them. For if the environment in the shape of parents or teachers could make a difference to the score, is the test valid? Is it still culture and experience free? Is this kind of figure any use at all?

An IQ test may be used to show the difference in a dyspraxic child's academic status and his 'performance IQ' or results on tests which measure competence in motor tasks. Such 'evidence' is often required when specialist help is sought, but such results really just give an indication of events at one moment in time. Those in authority who organise extra help in schools however, may need such figures to claim extra assistance.

Influences on intelligence

Once again, to try to explain intelligence, we need to confront the nature/nurture issue. Is intellectual capacity inherited and therefore largely fixed or is it amenable to change and if so, what part does the environment play?

Heredity

Many psychologists who believe that IQ is inherited base much of their evidence on twin studies. Brody (1992) studied identical twins reared together in a shared environment, and found the scores of their intelligence correlated at .85, a very high score. Identical twins reared apart, and so subject to different environmental influences, still showed a high score, i.e. between .60-.70 in different studies. These high correlations indicate a strong genetic component. Similarly, studies of adopted children show that their IQ is nearer that of their birth parents than that of their adoptive ones. This would also support the nature/heredity/genetic stance.

Environment

What of the other camp then? What part does environment play? It is tremendously difficult to control factors in different groups of children so that findings can be generalised in any meaningful way. Capron and Duyme (1989) tried to do this by carrying out an extensive study which included children from all the social strata, i.e. from highly advantaged to severely disadvantaged families and from parents with high IQs to those with much lower scores. They found that there was a difference of 11 or 12 points for children reared in advantaged homes. This meant that environmental support could influence IQ.

Worldwide studies now apportion 50 per cent of the variation in IQ scores to heredity and the rest to environmental influence or the interaction of heredity and environment together. And so genes indicate a range of possible functioning, i.e. they give upper and lower boundaries, but the environment can significantly influence where, within that range, children can function. And so all those who interact with children, be they parents, teachers or carers, while not being able to produce a genius in every child, can give their children an 'environmental boost' so that they reach their potential. This means that although there may not be a large IQ change, their children will be better able to play the fullest role that they can, both in school and at home.

CHAPTER 5

Social development and making friends

The first relationships children have are with their parents, and clinics and reading materials all emphasise the importance of early bonding. Ainsworth (1972) identified this term and she defined it as, 'the strong and long lasting affectational tie formed between baby and parents'. She also held that if bonding did not happen, then later relationships could be affected. Immediately parents who considered that they had not been able to create this bond felt cheated or guilty or inadequate. Now the timing of bonding has been widened (Myers 1987). It is now thought to depend on 'the pattern of interlocking behaviours which develop over the first weeks and months' (Bee 1995). 'Having time' is a comfort for those who have fretful infants or premature babies which need intensive care and can't be at home in the early weeks.

Some dyspraxic babies are not easy to rear. Some are difficult to feed and this may cause them to be irritable, especially if they sense that their parents are tense, and some hardly need any sleep. 'She only ever slept for three hours at a time', explained one distraught mum. 'I'd spend hours persuading her to feed then she seemed to be awake again before I had everything tidied up. It was frantic!' This can put a strain on bonding especially if the parents think they must be doing something wrong or if they are disappointed or exhausted by the way their baby behaves. Another difficulty in forming relationships comes if the child does not or cannot hold eye contact and smile. These are particularly rewarding episodes for tired parents, but sadly many dyspraxic children avoid eye contact, so this way into bonding is lost. This communication, this mutuality appears to underlie much of the security and pleasure which parent and child derive from each other.

Some children just seem to be born with difficult temperaments and the wear and tear on parents is enormous especially if they have financial worries or are concerned that other parents seem to be managing much better. Perhaps the parents did not have a secure relationship with their parents themselves and are hoping to establish lots of immediate reciprocal love with their child. If the child doesn't seem to respond in the expected way, they feel they have failed. There are lots of reasons why the first months are difficult but secure relationships can still be built, perhaps best when expectations become realistic, when outside pressures are ignored and when everyone begins to relax and realise that learning to be a parent takes time and practice. It is important to persevere. Schaffer (1989) urges parents to do all they can to build a positive early relationship with their child, for 'the establishment of the child's primary social relationships are generally considered to constitute the foundation on which all psychosocial behaviour is based'.

How does this psychosocial behaviour develop? Fagot and Pears (1996) claim that children who have secure attachments at home are 'more likely to be altruistic or nurturant and create more reciprocal friendships'. But what if this doesn't happen? What if the child comes home from school and repeatedly says he has no friends?

One of the saddest things is to hear children say, 'No one will let me play', and this can worry parents more than any academic difficulties. The parents of dyspraxic children know their child is bright but they so want him to be happy at school, and that comes, they feel, from having friends. A tremendous feeling of helplessness comes with the realisation that many, if not most children with dyspraxia are destined to be loners or worse, the victim of bullies who pick on anyone they see as being different. Very often dyspraxic children, because of their impulsivity and having to be supervised all the time, are more sheltered at home than others in their peer group. They therefore face a bigger change when they come to school. If their planning skills are poor, they may have more difficulty visualising what the day holds and they will be tentative and possibly reluctant to join in. This can make them vulnerable and when they can't tie laces or play football or ride a bike either, all 'public' differences, then they tend to be left out. Jake found this. He explained, 'When we go the gym, no one will take me for a partner. If it's games, I play with the teacher usually or I have to go into a three and they sometimes look angry. Why am I always the last to be picked?'

Social skills too play a part, for when table manners become important and finger food no longer suffices as party fare, then the children who can't use a knife and fork or who spill and break things are left out and of course the children don't understand why. 'There's another party and I'm not invited again Mum, why not?'

When do these difficulties begin? Isolation may not be apparent at nursery, for at this stage children are egocentric, i.e. they are almost completely tied up in their own concerns. They play near one another rather than with one another in any real or sustained way. At this stage they have the language to make interactions happen, but not yet the empathy or sympathy to sustain them. They work in groups, perhaps baking cakes, but they are usually checking that they get their allotted turns rather than being worried about how anyone else is faring. Development however means change, and soon it is important to the children that they are welcomed as part of a group and a little later that they have a best friend.

The importance of being the same

Even in the first years at school, and parents say 'earlier and earlier', children want to be the same, hence the pleas for the same clothes and trainers, the same haircuts and computer games. They instinctively feel that this will help them to be one of the gang, a position which offers security and 'not being left out'. Few children have the courage to go out of their way to include a left out child, even though some who have a well developed sense of altruism know that they should. Nor do they want to be different in any other way. They want to conform to the current image and the popular craze whether it is being good at sport or being tall and thin – they want to be cool!

Children choose friends from those who are like them; they have a strong sense of 'them' and 'us' and will jealously guard against intrusion. Even in the younger age groups many children have strong stereotypes of those who are 'not like me'. This is why ethnic minority children gravitate to their own kind at seven or so (Aboud and Doyle 1995). This is quite natural, it seems, for the children are establishing the mores of their own culture. This solidarity is more evident with boys' groups especially when they are quite newly formed. This 'wanting to be part of a group' can even cause clever children to deliberately underachieve in school, as 'being different' means being left out. It is not difficult to see where parents' goals and children's ways diverge.

Choosing friends at an early age can depend on children's rather superficial judgments which cover concrete rather than abstract factors. Some fascinating research by Edinburgh students asked children of different ages to describe their best friend.

Example

Craig, aged six, volunteered to talk about Sam, his 'special friend'.

'He's a big big fellow – huge really, with big feet and he sometimes falls over and bangs into me. He has fair hair and usually is kind, but not always for we fall out. He has a rabbit and a dog and I wish I had one too. Sam stays in quite a wee house with a green door at the front . . .'

As you can see his comments were mainly about appearances – surface qualities rather than enduring factors. Gemma's account of her friend, Lynn, was quite different. She was 11.

Example

'I'll tell you about Lynn. She's my very best friend. She gets us all organised. She's the captain of our netball team and she's really dependable at turning up and giving her best shot. The good thing is that if we lose she doesn't blame one person because we are a team. That helps if the shooters have a bad day. She's not very clever but she copes and doesn't mind too much. She giggles a lot and keeps us all cheery.'

Gemma was much more concerned with attitudes and capabilities, i.e. deeper and more long-lasting attributes than those which concerned Craig, and these reports were typical of the children's comments at each age.

This could offer comfort to parents of dyspraxic children – friendship patterns may change once the children's deeper qualities become part of the equation. This will happen more readily if the children in the class have no established pecking order which has endured for some time, but nonetheless friendship patterns do change as the children mature.

Having the same interests

When children move beyond the boundaries of their family to find friends, the peer group becomes very important. At age six or seven, cooperative play develops with children playing together for some sustained time. At this age the activity the children prefer to do is very important. Bee (1999) tells us that, 'shared interests continue to form the major basis of these relationships'. And so, one way for adults to try helping children who don't get to play, is to find the kind of thing they really enjoy doing and then plan how this could be introduced into the curriculum, or find ways in which the child might be able to join others who also like that kind of activity at recreation times.

This sounds straightforward, but of course the child who has caused all this concern may not want to join the children who are engrossed in his kind of activity. He may know exactly who he wants to join and be willing to risk rejection rather than settling for another group of children. Liam did this. Although his teacher knew he was very interested in animals – and asked him to bring in his favourite book to share with a group of children who enjoyed animals too – this didn't work because Liam still wanted to be a part of the dominant group in the class, i.e. the group he saw as being made up of the popular children.

This activity-based strategy very often does help however, and the planning involves:

- finding the child's interests and preparing a new initiative based on that, (this is so that the child doesn't have the difficulty of breaking into an already established game), then
- setting up the appropriate resources, hoping that interested children will come to play or, if that fails, inviting a group of like-minded children to join in.

But why should some children's company be sought and others shunned?

The characteristics of popular and rejected children

Some of the qualities which cause children to be left out are beyond their control which seems most unfair. Physically larger, but slim, better looking children, especially if they have sunny temperaments, tend to be the most popular. Perhaps being popular allows them to smile more? It is difficult certainly for rejected children to smile; they are understandably sulky or aggressive or withdrawn – all factors which cause the rejection to be sustained. This is often the fate of obese children, as is name calling. These children are rejected and ridiculed and are often driven to seek comfort in eating more. Sadly, they sometimes have other negative qualities attributed to them as well – laziness and stupidity (Stunkard and Sobel 1995) – even when there is no evidence to bear this out. Seeing this happen, 'fear of being fat' can cause even children of eight or nine to diet.

Popular children are 'non-aggressive; they explain things; they take their playmates' views into consideration; they are able to regulate their expression of strong emotions' (Pettit *et al.* 1996). In other words they can read other people's reactions and adjust their own behaviour accordingly; they have a well developed emotional intelligence and are consistently positive. On the other hand, rejected children are often disruptive; they spoil games by being over loud and boisterous or, in an attempt to show power, they themselves reject children who offer to play. Dyspraxic children sometimes see aggression as the way to solve their difficulties. If they are involved in even a slight accident, they may interpret any bump as 'meant', i.e. as a deliberate act against them, and they retaliate in a hostile way in return. This just makes everything worse.

While children do offer support to their friends and develop empathy and altruism as they mature, they also tease, argue and fight, in other words they use aggressive behaviours. Some children will do this much more with their siblings at home – indeed parents with several youngsters sometimes compare their home territory to a war zone! Only children of course don't have this opportunity to try out different strategies for getting their own way and may save their aggression for school or they may retreat from the fray, unsure as to the consequences of becoming involved, or of course they may be naturally placid children. But patterns of aggression do change and there are important differences in the ways in which boys and girls vent their feelings.

Patterns of aggression
In the early years children are likely to use physical violence and they will hit out if their wishes are thwarted. But as their verbal skills improve, this method of retaliation diminishes and they use taunts or name calling instead. Boys in junior school relish competitiveness/dominance/physical aggression more than girls, a finding which endorses gender stereotyping. They tend to gather in larger groups and move further from home. None of these attributes is likely to help children with dyspraxia make friends. When Maccoby (1990) carried out her study of children making friends, she found that the patterns of interaction used by the two sexes were qualitatively different. Whereas girls used explanations and asked, 'Can I have a turn?', boys grabbed what they wanted, exclaiming, 'Give me that!' This may well explain why shy or introverted boys prefer to play with girls, for they feel unable to cope with aggressive behaviour.

Another pattern which is not popular is coercive behaviour, where children use emotional blackmail to gain what they want. Other children recognise this, and while they may applaud it in a popular child who uses it infrequently to gain an advantage for the group, they deride it in a less popular child who uses it to gain a personal advantage. If these children have been 'successful' at home, through building a coercive attachment pattern with their parents who perhaps want to compensate the child for not having friends at school, then the children will try this behaviour at school and be confused and distressed when it does not work. The trouble is that rejected children often find that the only group which welcomes them is made up of other rejected children, and the role model they provide may not be helpful at all.

And so children can inadvertently build barriers to friendship, and the sadness is that not getting to play at four often means the same at eight and ten. But this need not persist. Children can change their ways once they are able to understand that others have needs; once they are aware of the perspectives of others and how their own behaviour impacts on their chance of becoming an accepted member of the group. Some children, unhappily, find great difficulty in making this change.

Understanding other people's perceptions: the development of a theory of mind

At around two years of age, children begin to understand that other people have intentions and that their behaviour will mirror these, e.g. if a child looks longingly at a cake, the likelihood is that he will try to get it. By three this kind of understanding deepens – the children begin to develop theories, 'If that person believes this, he is likely to do this, or perhaps that'. They also start to realise that someone may still want something, even though he can't have it. The understanding however has not deepened to the extent that they realise that other people may act on beliefs that are incorrect.

At age four or five, there are still aspects of other people's thinking to be grasped. The four-year-old understands 'I know that you know', but does not appreciate that this process is reciprocal. Such understanding develops for most children around age five to seven. This is a critical stage in the development of genuine reciprocal friendship. If two children, at different levels of development and therefore understanding, try to make friends, it is not difficult to see how misunderstandings, which are developmental rather than intentional, arise. Most preschool children can accurately read the facial expressions for 'happy' or 'sad' but hardly any can deal with 'proud' or 'guilty'. This is complex enough for children without specific difficulties. How much harder it is for those who have real problems in this perceptual area, e.g. for children with autistic tendencies.

One piece of advice given to help these children, is to immerse them in social encounters so that they have plenty of opportunity to see different modes of interaction, for children without siblings and self-sufficient children who are content to play alone or in a very small group are more likely to have difficulty with interpretation of emotions and subsequent actions, than children who have a wider social group (Lewis 1990). The dilemma of artificially engineering sympathetic encounters against knowing that this is not reality, is a difficult one to resolve. Perhaps the answer is to take one stage at a time and above all to keep the interactions calm and stress free.

Example

One dad, Graeme, who had recently joined a self-help group, thought that having their children gathered together would be a good way for them to make friends, because 'they'd all have the same kinds of difficulties'. He thought there would be a shared understanding which would promote friendships. When he took his 11-year-old son, Kerr, to the group however, the lad retreated and just sat in a corner, overwhelmed by the size of the company and the noise. Graeme decided to persevere and after about six increasingly successful sessions his son volunteered to lead some of the craft activities. How had this happened? Graeme explained, 'One of the older children who was managing to overcome some of his own difficulties encouraged him and this was marvellous – I could have hugged that child. He comes regularly to play at our house now and although they still tend to play at different things, Kerr likes his stamp album while Gary prefers computer games, at least there are two of them together in the room and Kerr can tell everyone at school about "his friend". I don't think anyone who has not experienced it can understand the horror of the day when your child doesn't have friends.'

And so, although the boys were not playing together in any cooperating sense, they tolerated each other and respected what the other was trying to do. The important thing was that they were able to talk about 'my friend'. Both sets of parents reported the 'huge relief' that this brought. One dad explained that 'my whole day is a lot brighter. A dark cloud has lifted. I don't worry nearly so much now'.

Differences in children which make it difficult for them to play

Children with dyspraxia very often find it impossible to play games that others have planned. They have enough difficulty in planning what they themselves wish to do in a 'this then that' sequence of events. Given that this is problematic, they are even less likely to be able to interpret someone else's plans and appreciate the emotions that disrupting them could engender. Many games have unwritten rules; children just seem to absorb them from experience. For those who have not got this facility, sustaining friendships can be very difficult.

Children who can't do the movement skills which other children value, e.g. play football or ride a bike, tend to get left out when their more physically able friends abandon them. If they feel they have broken into a group and then they are left out again, this may well cause anxiety, even depression.

Children with ADHD (attention deficit hyperactivity disorder) have similar difficulties even though the cause is different. These children are extremely restless. This prevents concentration for themselves and causes disruption and annoyance to others. They have a deficit in the ability to inhibit behaviour; they must react to any stimulus. Their problem is much more severe than that of the 'normally' restless child who is often urged to sit still. When other children get angry at being disturbed, these children can't alter their behaviour to comply and resentment builds up. Sometimes naughty children will provoke them as a way of setting up a distraction in the class. Their high level of impulsivity and lack of ability to concentrate also means that they cannot participate in any sustained game.

It is not surprising to find that many children who can't make friends display excessive aggressiveness. Unfortunately, this compounds their difficulty. This combination may well lead to them bullying or being bullied. Delinquency is sometimes the resort of children who are miserable and withdrawn. They 'get back' at society by showing disdain for its rules. This is one way of making sense of their existence.

On a much less sombre note, some dyspraxic children take the content of conversations too literally; they don't see the joke or appreciate the innuendo. One boy explained, 'I see them all laugh, so I go "Ha Ha" too, but I really don't know why!' Teasing can be especially hurtful for these children, who, unable to understand laughing with others, certainly won't be able to laugh at themselves. They also have difficulty realising that some comments are not meant to be taken literally, but shrugged off, not to be taken to heart. If the offending child is then taken to task, resentment builds up. This is the kind of situation that leads to children being avoided and acts against children being able to make friends. How do adults begin to explain this to children?

Children with any kind of learning difficulty often have related social problems which make matters worse. The trouble is that because they are individuals with their own personality factors and because they are brought up in different environments with different value systems and cultural practices, there is no one recipe which will be guaranteed to help them all.

Mixed age classrooms

McClelland and Kinsey (1996) offer one solution. They found that if children experiencing difficulties in making friends could be incorporated into classes with younger children, the problem was often eased. These younger children did not make the same social demands. Moreover, they respected the older ones simply because of their age, and there was a chance for a new, positive start. Parents of dyspraxic youngsters often find that their children prefer the company of younger ones. A small school with several age groups together could well help.

Parenting styles

The family plays a vital role in the social development of their children. Knowing this, parents of dyspraxic children often wonder if they have done something wrong. 'Did I not pay enough attention, or give too much?' are commonly asked questions. The answer usually is that concerned parents are not to blame, they have done all they can. There is no universal recipe which will guarantee success in bringing up any child and this may be because the children interacting with their parents present a unique set of characteristics. Families which have positive, helpful children however would usually claim to have provided an environment which shows:

- warmth or nurturance;
- appropriately high expectations;
- honest interactions;
- consistent standards and rules.

This consistency is vitally important to dyspraxic children because of their difficulty in understanding and adapting to change. Established routines allow dyspraxic children to help especially in everyday tasks where they have learned the procedures that earn them praise. For this reason, some prefer to stay indoors at playtime especially when they have the legitimate excuse of helping the teacher. This is a kindly way to relieve some of the pressure of the day, because these children feel secure indoors where they know the routine. This also saves the miseries of donning outdoor wear then changing back within a short time and finding once more that they don't get to play.

But of course not all children develop in the same ways and this is as true for children with dyspraxia as any other. Some are anxious to take every learning opportunity while others are reluctant and shy. The effects from the children's environment are complex and pervasive. Schools must try to understand the implications of disabilities and compensate for any disadvantages so that the children have the best possible chance to realise their potential. These are not easy things to do.

As children from many different backgrounds come together into school to undertake their education, they are entering a new world of different demands and complex 'rules'. Children with dyspraxia need extra time and space to let them understand and realise that they will be able to cope. The staff too have a myriad of demands based on decentring, i.e doing their best to understand each child's participation in the fascinating process that is learning.

Being bullied

Having few friends is bad enough but no child should have to tolerate being bullied, yet this often happens whenever a vulnerable child is seen as being different. Perhaps the dyspraxic children's inability to share jokes because they take conversations too literally or their sometimes erratic or inappropriate behaviour sets them apart and they make easy targets. By the middle years of childhood, children are old enough to realise the implications of their behaviour on others and vindictive children can spark off scenes when they know other children will be blamed. Even when this is recognised and the real perpetrators are named, some will say they are sorry while others show no remorse at all. Some children will remain impassive even in the face of the other children's distress and some even retaliate by being even more aggressive later. Observations like this cause us to ask if such aggressive children are hostile all of the time or if their attitude is context specific? If teachers can find out what is causing the anger and correct it, will all be well? Dunn and Kendrick (1982) found that although many children could be both sunny and hostile, there were children who 'responded to their siblings' distress with glee, and never, ever moved to comfort'. A chilling thought.

From this research, we can gather that some children learn how to inflict hurt but never learn to sympathise. Sometimes explanations of bad behaviour, e.g. 'You mustn't hit because it is really painful', can even stimulate further aggression towards the damaged child. And so no one can expect all children to develop altruism, or even with explanation, develop caring and sympathetic ways. Sadly, bullies can attract other children who decide to join them simply to stop themselves becoming a target. There are many policies on bullying now. Where can help be found?

Where to get help

The Dyspraxia Foundation in 'Seeing your way through' (1998) offers practical advice to children who have been bullied and to their parents. This is because inappropriate and possibly emotional intervention can make things worse, yet how can parents stand by and do nothing? The children are advised to write down or have someone else scribe the events which occurred. This is so that they can recount them to someone they trust without getting flustered and so losing the sequence of what occurred. When the bullying is actually taking place, they are advised to keep calm and only repeat a statement which they have practised beforehand, saying for example, 'My name is Helen. I don't want any other name', or 'I want you to leave me alone'. They must not be goaded into retaliating, either verbally or physically. The main advice is to tell someone trustworthy in authority – then these people must take steps, they are legally bound to do so. It may help children to know that 15 per cent of all children are bullied. While this is a sad indictment of our young people, the figures show the child that he is not alone and very importantly, that he is not to blame.

Many children will try to hide the fact that they are being bullied because 'at school no one has time to listen', and at home, 'Mum'll go up to school and the others will know it's me that's told', or 'You just have to put up with it. My Dad says he was bullied too'. The above reasons show why many parents are uneasy, even afraid that going to school will make things worse for their child. But if they do nothing the bullies have won. And if the school does not take steps to help, then action should be taken against them too. Sometimes schools are unaware that bullying is going on and indeed some children can be oversensitive to a single playground remark. But when aggression, likely to be verbal rather than physical in the six to eleven age range, is happening regularly and if the child is affected through crying or being withdrawn or having pains or wanting to go home, these signs must be investigated. Sometimes bullies are being bullied themselves and are venting their own power over a fearful child. Very often they are insecure themselves. Whatever the reason they cannot be allowed to harm other children. Parents should ask to see the school's policy on bullying and then they will be able to identify issues which are not being checked. This can provide a focus for discussion with the head teacher. It also helps parents to stay less emotional and therefore more able to present their case. All of this takes courage, but if the parents are afraid and hesitate, then they must imagine and take the blame for the effect continued bullying has on their child.

Of course many bullies are too devious to be caught and may accost the vulnerable children once they have left school. If this happens, the school may feel that they cannot take the responsibility for what goes on outside their premises. The only solution is to have the child met and inform the police. The bullied child may not want this, but he has to be kept safe.

Developing empathy

It is apparent then that children differ in the extent to which they can empathise with the feelings of another child and that some simply cannot appreciate another child's distress when they themselves do not feel it. They therefore cannot appreciate the perspective of another person. Different children have different levels of emotional development just as they differ intellectually or in their movement skills. But emotional development is awesome, in that failure to develop hurts others and eventually the children themselves. Some children of course have aggressive role models and may be copying patterns of behaviour they see at home. If these children can be helped to decentre, i.e. to understand the implications of their actions for others and realise that in the longer term their peers will resent their behaviour, then perhaps they may try to change. This can be attempted through classroom discussions in a personal and social development programme or through role play in drama, when the suspected bully may take the place of his tormented 'friend'.

The capacity to understand that someone else is happy or sad or proud of some achievement brings with it an appreciation of 'why', i.e. the underlying events that have caused that emotion. If they appreciate someone else's emotion, do they feel it themselves? The answer could be 'yes' or 'no' depending on the type of event as well as the personality of the child. Think of watching a sad film. Children and adults weep when 'ET' goes home or when 'The Snowman' melts. They know it is just a story and yet emotions overtake cold logic. The audience has empathised; they have felt the emotions of the characters in the play. The film makers have portrayed experiences which children can relate to quite easily, and adults can remember with nostalgia – all that is required is a 'temporary suspension of disbelief in the fiction that has been created' (Harris 1992). Is this what drama in school tries to do? Is the aim to encourage a deeper understanding of other people's feelings and through that their lives? Can children really understand what it is like to be someone else, perhaps a child who has dyspraxia, or is this a charade? Do they need experiences or can they imagine the implications in their heads? If they can't, how are they to learn to empathise with those that are less fortunate than themselves? Is there any real hope of beating the bullies till they do?

Developing prosocial or altruistic behaviour

The development of altruism or prosocial behaviour shows age changes just as all other aspects of development do. Altruism is 'intentional voluntary behaviour intended to benefit another' (Eisenberg 1992), and usually this is at some cost to oneself.

Example

A small piece of research illustrates this well. Children of different ages were told a story and then asked separately, 'If you were there, what would you do?'

The story:

> You are rollerblading through the park with your friends on the way to a pizza place where you will all have tea. On the way you see a boy/girl who has fallen and is hurt. If you were there, what would you do?

(The researchers found that it was important to offer a boy or a girl as the injured one in the story, as one girl, in a pilot study which only had only included boys, replied, 'I'd do nothing – I hate all boys!' With this adjustment, the replies from children in the subsequent study were fascinating and clearly showed how altruism developed over the junior years.

Children's replies

Alice aged four:

> 'Well . . . well, I'm really wee and if I saw a policeman I'd tell him. But I couldn't wait to help because I'd get lost.'

Alice wasn't really going to help for the very understandable and legitimate reason of 'getting lost', but she was aware that she should do something – tell a policeman!

Jimmy aged six:

'I'd give him my blades to get home. He'd have to write down his address. But then I'd not be able to keep up with my pals – no wait. I'd help him over to the park bench and then a grown up would see him.'

Jimmy knew he should help. He was able to conceptualise a plan – even though he hadn't thought of how an injured child could use his blades. He already had a street wise attitude – the boy might steal his blades – and in the end, concern for himself won!

Rob aged nine:

'I'd pick him up and put him on my back and we'd go to the pizza place because I would have enough money to pay for us both, or I'd phone his home on my mobile and tell his mother where he was . . . Then I'd catch up on the others.'

Rob had two strategies to help. He obviously preferred the second, but given that he couldn't make contact with the boy's mother, he was prepared not to abandon the child. Altruism is growing.

Rebecca aged eleven:

'I'd first of all check how badly he was hurt and if it was serious I'd get someone to phone for an ambulance. If it was a sprain I'd just wait with her till someone came along or she was able to put her weight on it.' Asked if she wouldn't mind missing her treat she said, 'Oh no,' and she looked quite superior, knowing that she had said the 'right thing'. Then she spoiled it somewhat, by adding, 'I hate pizza anyway!'

Rebecca had a much clearer idea of what society expected and she was prepared to fulfil that role. She had thought about the situation much more than the others, in that she considered different degrees of hurt, and was ready to have someone phone for an ambulance. She was totally confident and in charge of events. Do you think she was envisaging other kinds of spin·offs for herself, perhaps relaying the story later and being applauded or seeing inside the A and E department? Or was she prepared to give up her treat with no thought of gain for herself? This would be the case in real altruism!

This was just a practical, 'research' way of checking out the claims about the age-related development of altruism made in the literature. But why should children respond in different ways? Does their society and/or their culture influence their behaviour? Would the overt things the children said they would do, have happened in reality?

Eisenberg (1992) explains that very young children of three or so, will offer a toy or cuddle to another child who has been hurt. They will wrap their arms around and murmur soothing words. These children are just beginning to understand about the emotions of others and are newly able to respond to them. Older children offer more in the way of toys or material comforts but less physical contact. (Rob's picking the child up was a means of transport, not comfort!) Do these gestures mirror practices at home? Perhaps these deliberations and actions reflect the parents' ways of giving reassurance, i.e. with less physical contact as their children mature? There may be a gender difference here – certainly more boys tend to shy way from overt, especially public demonstrations of emotion. The different ways families show emotion must influence the children's behaviour, and of course this may be the mode of the specific cultural group as well. And so there are many influences, and it is not easy to understand where they have come from or interpret exactly what they mean.

This brings us back to the question of teachers 'sorting out' bullying. What are they to do if they are faced with two accounts of what went on? They may suspect what actually happened, but if they were not there, they have no evidence to prove or disprove what they have been told. But at the very least they should make accurate notes describing both sides of the story. These notes should tell exactly what occurred and who was involved. Then a record exists. Later incidents may substantiate earlier claims.

Children with dyspraxia may not fully appreciate the subtleties which come with emotional development. Parents are therefore urged:

- Create a warm, loving climate, and say, 'Let's have a happy, quiet time together'. This shows the child that his company is important to you, especially when he is good.
- Explain the best way to respond in different situations. Make up stories like the pizza one, (see Example above) and discuss the implications of several hypothetical replies. Don't take it for granted that the child will absorb and copy the family's way of behaving. Explain that, 'It's always best to be helpful because you will feel good too' or 'Jane is sad today because her dog has died. Stay with her quietly. Don't speak about Toby – just be there for her, and she'll know you care'.
- Give lots of praise immediately after the event and say why it has been earned. Not 'Good chap' but 'Good for you tidying your room without being asked. That's a big help'. This is much more likely to reinforce the behaviour and for it to happen again. This is especially important if the praise has to come some time after the event because the short term memory difficulty can cause children to forget. In that case, 'That's good' loses impact, because the child does not remember how the praise was earned.
- Provide opportunities for children to do helpful things. In today's climate of rushing everywhere, it can be so much easier and quicker, and possibly cheaper (because of breakages!) just to do the jobs yourself. But obvious jobs left undone can help the child to contribute and let him see that you can be 'forgetful' or a bit slapdash too! A 'buddy atmosphere' can change the power status and make it easier for children who know they are often inept to take part in the daily routine. This also allows them to practise their coping skills.
- Be a generous, helpful role model. Dyspraxic children find it easier to do as you do rather than what they know you should do! This is because they may well have difficulty fitting the correct actions to different situations.

Interpreting and analysing and responding to emotional behaviour is difficult and upsetting when it goes wrong. How much more difficult is it for children with dyspraxia who lack the facility to interpret others' cues?

CHAPTER 6

Emotional development

The self-concept

Everyone hopes that their children will be happy and confident and be able to make the most of all the opportunities that come their way. To do this they need to have a positive self-concept. When children have a disability, their families are naturally very concerned that their children's self-concept will be harmed. What do they mean? Why should this happen? What will the implications be? These are important questions for all those who interact with children, especially those with any kind of difficulty, for they are likely to be the most sensitive and vulnerable, possibly even seeing slights where none was intended. Certainly if people concentrate on children's difficulties without producing appropriate learning materials so that the children can succeed and thus have lots of genuine positive feedback, their opinion of themselves will not be high.

What then is the self-concept?

Self-concept is the name given to the picture children build of themselves through their interactions with others. This picture is formed as a result of quite an intricate, ongoing evaluation, sometimes called a tri-dimensional image. This is explained by the words, 'What I think of myself depends on what I think you think of me!'

Cooley (1962) called this 'the looking glass self', a name which describes the reflective process which is involved. And just as the mirror can give a flattering picture at times and a distorted, disappointing one at others, the self-concept tends to fluctuate in children, not really becoming relatively firmly fixed until age eighteen or so when the young adults are through adolescence – a time of uncertainty comparable to the terrible twos! Moreover, the picture is subdivided.

While the self-concept is the picture itself, the self-esteem comes from the value the person gives to that picture. It is a global evaluation of one's own worth. It is the distance between the perceived self and the ideal self as shown in Figure 6.1 below.

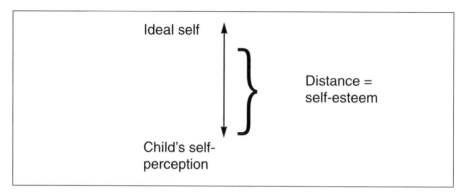

Figure 6.1 Self-esteem

How does that come about? How does the child fix this important picture of himself? Harter (1990) tells us that the child's self-esteem is 'the product of two internal assessments or judgments'. Each child gauges some discrepancy between what he thinks he is like, and what he thinks he *ought* to be like, or what he would like to be. If there is just a short gap between the two, the child's self-esteem will be high. If, however, the distance is large, his self-esteem will be low. The dyspraxic child may well feel inadequate or diminished if he thinks his clumsiness and social inadequacies are detrimental to his standing in the eyes of the important people around him, and indeed Harter points out the importance of the support children have from parents and friends. Now the dyspraxic child knows full well that he has difficulties, there is no use pretending they don't exist. But the children have to be sure that they are loved despite them, or better still loved even more because of them – they have to be told they are special possibly more often than other children because they are more liable to be hurt by uncaring or unknowing others. Children who feel that others like them, will have a higher self-esteem than if they doubt whether they do.

A further important point is that the children's self-concept is more likely to be affected by those they respect. If someone they don't approve of or don't care for offers a compliment or a diminishing comment they will not be particularly affected. They will be more able to shrug it off. They will more readily accept what people they look up to say as being true. These 'most important people' change at least temporarily. Firstly parents, then teachers, then the peer group, then celebrities for fashion or lifestyle, appear as important role models. There are obvious implications for those who know they are influential in allowing the children to build a confident picture of their abilities.

Vulnerable children are hurt by the bullies but don't really believe their taunts unless they are carried on for some time or unless other children join in. Then self doubts are reinforced, 'They can't all be wrong, can they?' This is one reason why it is vital to stop bullying as fast as possible. Children with dyspraxia tend to take statements at face value, i.e. quite literally. Innuendoes are not understood and double meanings and sarcasm only confuse. Interestingly children with an obvious or severe handicap are not prone to be bullied – possibly this is why children with dyspraxia, a 'hidden handicap' (Kirby 1999a), fare worse.

As they form their self-esteem, children set their own goals. The picture of the 'ideal' is not the same for every child. Some value academic work (intellectual goals), and wish to shine at that, while others value prowess in sports (perceptual-motor goals), or having good friends (social goals), even being able to be confident and 'cool' (emotional goals). When they anticipate, or experiences and interactions tell them, that they are not going to achieve these goals at the level they would wish, then their self-esteem can take a nasty knock. Of course, nearly all children are the same in this respect, for not many achieve to their early dreams of becoming a world champion racing driver or a prima ballerina. But when all things are equal, when children have no obvious limiting difficulties, realisation can take longer to set in and by this time other interests and opportunities may have taken their place.

Children with dyspraxia, however, are likely to realise sooner that their potential in several fields is reduced and that even with practice some goals are unobtainable. When children see themselves as failing to live up to their own goals, they need extra support and help. One would think that comfort statements such as, 'But look how good you are at your music, let's practise that and then you can play at the school concert' would help to compensate, but they only do so if the child values that activity himself – if that fits his framework of worthwhile things to do. Otherwise ideas are likely to be rejected and parents feel helpless, not knowing what to suggest.

Having said that, some children can show extreme commitment to achieving their preferred aim and overcome huge obstacles to do it, so parents have to try to assess the child's determination, try to provide resources (could outside agencies help?) that make achievement possible, or be ready with alternative suggestions which if possible link to the child's original idea of what he wants to do or be. Parents could seek out subtler ways of helping, to avoid causing the child stress – possibly making a tape recording of stories or plays, possibly devising computer games, possibly sending craft work in to *Blue Peter*, whatever will show the child he can succeed and so build the child's confidence.

A negative impact on self-esteem happens when children perceive that they have failed to live up to their family's expectations, even worse when they consider that their family's support is contingent upon them reaching some goal. And so the children are afraid to tell that they have poor marks or no friends or are being bullied or haven't a place in the school team. Even though these things may not be the children's fault, in their own eyes they are culpable. And of course, admitting them is so painful. Children will often be heard denying or disputing reality, to try to retain a level of standing in their parents' eyes.

An important other component of the self-concept is 'body image', i.e. how children perceive their bodies and how nearly that matches their ideal – usually the 'cool', tall, slim, talented child. Children are surrounded by such images in magazines and on the media and if they don't see themselves as looking like that, their estimation of their own self-worth is diminished. This is particularly so if the children are by nature vulnerable and ambivalent about themselves. Unfortunately this can cause overeating for comfort. The children know that this will make the discrepancy worse and so feel guilty as well as greedy – or alternatively defiant, not caring – in other words they use denial strategies to help them cope, at least temporarily. This denial is a huge part of anorexia which can be the way some children respond. This usually has an intrinsic psychological basis which manifests itself in refusing to eat and being unable to realise the degree of emaciation which occurs. Those who are affected by this condition can weigh 5 stones and believe themselves fat.

Peer pressure to conform has a big effect on self-esteem. Children who deviate from the group's unwritten norms are likely to feel inadequate. Labels and judgments from others play a vital role in the formation of the self-concept. To a very large extent 'we come to think of ourselves what others think of us' (Cole 1991). This picture is derived from many sources, even unwitting remarks. Cole gives a good example. The child who comes home with a report card with 3s or 4s whose parents, thinking they are being supportive say, 'That's just fine – we didn't expect you to get 1s,' is left with a clear message about the parents' expectations! Of course, 'Why didn't you get 1s?' could have been even harder to handle! Dyspraxic children are likely to have widely diverging grades across the curriculum and parents will be able to point out that, 'That's you: the good ones, and that's your dyspraxia: the poorer ones', for surely sensitive teachers will have added a word of explanation? Perhaps they will have used alternative strategies as part of the assessment package, e.g. tape recorded stories, sums written out so that the children have only to concentrate on the answers which have to be filled in. In this case, there may be no poor grades or negative-sounding comments at all. In Scotland's primary schools the system of levels with each child working towards or attaining a level (which has pre-set achievement criteria) is accompanied by a teacher's statement, so the difficulties of reporting accurately and fully for dyspraxic children should be reduced.

The self-concept is gradually formed from these experiences but is not set in stone. It is responsive to changes in others' judgments and to the children's own successes. But once it is firmed up, it is relatively enduring, made more so by the fact that children will be likely to choose activities that confirm a negative model, 'I can't do that , I'm no use at it'. The trouble is that some children will generalise this model so that they feel they are no use, not only at the particular activity, but no use at all. This is a global self-concept: 'I'm good' or 'I'm a failure!' And once this idea has been reinforced by other 'failing' experiences – and the children may have selected these as a way to confirm the negative expectations they have of themselves – then depression may set in and remain through childhood and adolescence, even into adulthood. Counselling will try to effect change but the most vulnerable do not find it easy to believe what others say when lots of other circumstances have proved their own self-belief to be correct.

One answer for the general population of children is to give them lots of varied experiences so that they will build a balanced profile of their own abilities and have several successes within that. The idea is, that they will select the 'best' and be proud of those achievements. Dyspraxic children who do not transfer learning from one situation to another will not find this mix easy to cope with. Life is easier for them when they can choose what they want to do. For no one *has* to play football or have neat handwriting or be able to sing. Perhaps we need to identify the essentials – the daily life skills – concentrate on teaching these as priority, then beyond that, let the children choose?

Enhancing children's self-concept

Giving praise

This book has emphasised the importance of giving positive feedback or praise especially to children with difficulties, so that their self-concept will be enhanced. But how is this best done? Do we simply tell children 'That's good' and leave it at that or are there helpful strategies to help us know what to do and ways that could be self-defeating?

Very young children will accept unrealistic praise. They will be delighted by any form of gratification. They move on quickly from one activity to the next and may not pause to think whether what they have produced merits what they have been told. But older children are likely to feel that unwarranted praise is demeaning. They are perfectly well able to evaluate their work and if this disappoints them, then they are not likely to accept someone else's judgment, except perhaps in a borderline case. What they may do is lose respect for the one who offers the praise. The point is, that if children have any difficulties, their learning has to be structured into appropriate bite-size pieces so that with effort, the children can deserve praise. Children need genuine praise for progress that they can see. If teachers offer *realistic* praise the children know that their difficulties are understood.

Margaret Pope (1988), a head teacher of a school for children with learning difficulties, explains,

> I have been amazed at how well a child responds to an acceptance of his or her difficulties when this is coupled with a programme of positive activities that will lead to improvements. Telling a child he is good at something when as an intelligent human being he knows he's not, far from raising his self-esteem only reduces it.

This sentiment says 'be realistic but encouraging' and with dyspraxic children their intellectual capacity makes this perfectly possible. The intelligence however lets the children evaluate their 'product' against that of other children and frustration may result. Children have told me that 'Once I knew I had dyspraxia, I knew I wasn't stupid and that there would be things I could do well. It must be dreadful for children who can't manage anything at all really. How must they feel?' Reactions like this would seem to endorse labelling. Given a recognised label, the child then has a reason for his difficulties – one which has nothing to do with intelligence.

Example

One 12-year-old explained, 'This smart Alex guy said to me, "Come on slow coach, what's keeping you?" I said "Dyspraxia" – he said "What's that?" – I said "Go and find out, you ninny!"' – which shows that, given a label, these children can retaliate, maybe not too politely either!

Dyspraxic children may well have difficulty pacing their effort. This means that they may not finish or may rush the last part spoiling the effect, just to be finished in time. This means that formative assessment with praise which also contains some ongoing guidance is the best way.

Example

The colours you have chosen are really effective . . . your picture is coming on well. Remember to keep the design clear – don't spoil what you have done by making it fussy. You have 10 minutes to complete this part today. Let's set the timer. You'll need to put your painting on the drying screen before you tidy up the paints and water.

In this kind of scenario the children have praise and clear guidance about what to do next. The awareness of time problem is eased by the large egg timer which the child will turn over after it is empty – five minutes – and know that half the time has gone. The organisation of subsequent events, i.e. putting the painting aside before clearing away the water, will hopefully prevent disasters. A kindly 'buddy' nearby could be appointed to oversee these arrangements for the child if those instructions were too complex to be retained.

It is interesting to find that children with low self-esteem may rebuff praise, denying that they have made any improvement at all. If there is evidence of progress, they'll say, 'That was luck' rather than 'I did it better'. Are they so unused to praise that they can't believe others mean it? If their evaluation of themselves is 'fixed', this may be so. This means that parents and teachers have to spell out progress for these children or else they may not realise it, even choose not to recognise they have made it at all.

One fascinating piece of research by Gurney (1987) asked teachers to teach children to praise each other, but not in the way circle time does (because in my view that kind of praise can lose meaning because it is decontextualised – at least for the dyspraxic children – and being out of context causes children to say things like 'I like your hair' which doesn't hold much encouragement or in many cases even ring true). One way which was tried and evoked meaningful results is described now.

Example

First of all the children knew this was going to happen and they were allowed to choose what bit of work was to be shared. There were no unexpected surprises – children had time to plan and select. Then, two children (who were paired sensitively) had to look at each other's work closely and say one good thing about it. Sometimes this was, 'I can read it easily', a wonderful accolade for children who had difficulty with their writing skills or who often had letters out of order, or they made a comment about the imaginative content, e.g. 'That's good about Bob (the dog in one child's story), it makes me want to read on to find out if he gets out of the cave'. The comment might also be about the vocabulary, 'You have used some of the words we learned at drama'.

This kind of peer praise was found to be really effective. Moreover it reinforces the teaching points for all of the children. They can all join in and when the criteria concern 'good story lines' rather than neatness, the dyspraxic child's story can very often be the one read out to the class. As different children give their feedback, the teachers can see if the children choose to use the criteria that they themselves would apply and this can be very revealing as to whether the teaching points have been taken on board. Teachers who have tried this tell me this approach works best when it happens quite infrequently, when the children have had some advance notice and when they themselves have discreetly checked that the pieces of work have items which the assessing children can identify. If these can be 'new' things, this prevents repetition and keeps the activity alive.

These evaluations offer a useful strategy to find alternative ways of giving praise and endorse the claims made in Child's (1986) 'drive reduction theory' which gives an illustration to help clarify the points he makes. (Figure 6.2)

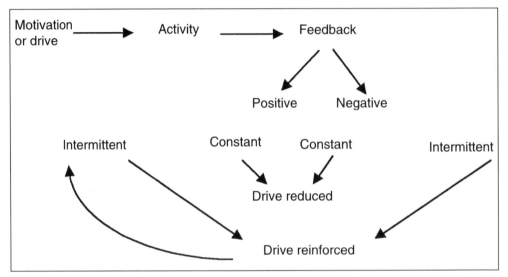

Figure 6.2 The drive reduction theory

The arrows show that when the aims of the teaching or the game or whatever are consistently met then interest and motivation are lost. Perhaps this is why golf stays as a long time challenge – even the experts cannot have a perfect round each time. And even when they are experts, new challenges arise when a different course means an unfamiliar environment. Perhaps this explains why playground games are all the rage, then, as suddenly they disappear. The children who can do them well get unremitting positive feedback which loses impact and those who have never managed abandon the game anyway. For classroom sustainment, having varying levels of praise intermittently seems to be the way to keep children on task. Teachers have to be psychologists too !

But of course praise need not be verbal from another person. Satisfaction in the activity is a kind of praise in itself – if not for progress then certainly for commitment.

The importance of practice

> **Example 18**
>
> One little girl, Coral, had severe perceptual-motor problems. Her balance was so poor that she often tipped off her seat. When she sat for any length of time she collapsed into herself and she did her writing leaning flat on her desk with her head turned to face the page. I was asked to try to find out what was wrong and so I carried out an assessment using a number of 'fun-to-do' activities. Coral, at 12 years old, couldn't manage any of these with any degree of success until it came to catching a ball. She could catch from any angle, even with one hand, even with her non-preferred hand (although she had little sense of hand dominance). She had found balancing possible by having her feet wide apart and intermittently leaning against a wall. Her ball skills provided a real opportunity for congratulations! Coral explained the reason why, 'Well at home, every night I play against the wall!'

This was a lovely illustration of the effectiveness of sustained and regular practice. The words sustained – for 15 minutes at a time – and regular – four times daily – are the critical ones here. Obviously Coral was having lots of positive feedback from this activity and it had not yet reached saturation point possibly because she often set herself new challenges such as having jingles which meant the ball activity had to be rhythmical – even trying two balls, or in Coral's parlance, 'doublies!' (For further activities see Appendices 2–4)

But how do parents and teachers encourage children who have no interest in some fundamental skill to practise it? Long-term goals are not effective motivators so the activity has to be broken down. If this still doesn't motivate the child, is it possible to relate the competences which are being practised to something the child would like to do better? Walking along a bench in the gym can be pretty boring and not give much incentive to 'push the head high', but if the child understands that this is an important way to help him balance and that 'looking ahead, not down at your feet' is really 'a practice for pedalling your bike' because 'when you are riding your bike, you can't look down or you'll not see where you are going', then the child might be more inclined to try. And so the key factors in successful practice are to do it:

- in short spells – 15 minutes or so at a time;
- regularly – four times a day, and possibly at the same time of day for severe difficulties;
- with explanations why – so that the child
(a) understands how best to cooperate, and
(b) appreciates the possible outcome, i.e. what 'other things' he will be enabled to do.

CHAPTER 7

Practical considerations for parents and teachers

When parents of dyspraxic children were asked to say what criteria they would use to choose a school, they said:

- a warm welcoming atmosphere, a caring ethos;
- friendly staff – people who have time to listen and who want to understand;
- a uniform of polo shirts and pull-on sweaters – no ties, no laces, no buttons;
- away from a busy road;
- near home to avoid bus journeys.

The first three were the key criteria. League tables were not important to any of the parents. 'We can cope with lots of things,' the parents explained, 'if the teachers will only be allowed time to listen.'

This list of practical strategies has come from the preceding chapters where the implications of children's difficulties have been explained. And just as individual children have different symptoms of dyspraxia with different levels of severity, the strategies to help them must be individually selected too. Parents and teachers know their children well. They know what kinds of help children are likely to accept and what kinds of intervention could make them feel worse. If children even know that everything possible is being done and that people are doing their best, they are more likely to accept that they must play a part in trying things out and sharing their thoughts about the helpfulness or otherwise of the strategies that have been tried. Communication between parents and teachers is imperative if the children are not to be confused by different signals, different value systems and different expectations.

Advice to parents, teachers and policy makers

The education authorities must play their part in helping dyspraxic children. Teachers do not have endless time or resources. Special equipment such as inclined boards for reading and writing make a huge difference to the children – they are not very expensive and they just have to be supplied, or else some children will have major difficulties. Inclusion doesn't just mean everyone together, it implies a humane learning environment where children with special needs have them recognised and where resources are such that the best opportunity for learning is provided. While parents should not have to pay for any resources, they may wish to do so if help from the authorities is delayed. They would then remain as the property of the child, going home at weekends or holidays. On the other hand, inclined boards and wobble boards can be improvised quite cheaply and if there are dads who are joiners or have DIY skills, perhaps they would be prepared to help. Class fund raising could also help the other children to understand and it is good for them to play a positive part in rallying round to help their less fortunate friend.

If the child needs to take tests for school reasons, he will be entitled to have more time than other children, to have questions or maps blown up (and this may necessitate a bigger desk to support them) or to have a scribe. Well before the test, the child needs to practise with items in similar enlarged sizes and with someone scribing for him. Several ways of helping the child gauge the passing of time may also be required. Any test will be harrowing enough without surprises.

Practical strategies to help

1. At school
2. Getting ready for school
3. At home

At school

The learning environment
Ensure that the children have an uninterrupted view of the board.

Remove distractors whenever possible – if not, make sure dyspraxic children are away from problems such as noise from computers, children passing, trees at windows, noises from the dining hall or other classrooms, in fact anything which will distract them and spoil their concentration. It would be an advantage for such children to be seated a little distance from others, if the child cannot bear his personal space to be invaded.

Check that the children can sit comfortably, well supported in suitable chairs. Hard chairs with metal legs tend to tip easily and this makes balance very difficult. If balance is a problem, sitting on the floor is not easy — it may even be painful. Allow the children to lean against a support and don't expect them to sit too long in one position.

Desks should be at elbow height. Small children benefit from a step if the desks are too high. Dangling legs pull the body forward over the desk and as they don't give support, this makes control of pencils or shifting papers difficult.

Give an inclined board for writing and reading. This eases tracking from the board to the jotter when writing. The angle also eases pressure on the wrist and allows the pen or pencil to flow. The inclined board also helps reading because the eyes are less likely to jump over letters. For children who need to press hard to obtain feedback from their proprioceptors, avoid pencils that break easily. Allow children to try out various pencil sizes to see which suits their individual grip. Triangular grips help some but not all children.

Check that any overhead light does not glare or reflect on the children's work. This exacerbates visual difficulties and can be very irritating for children who already have difficulty focusing and retaining their place on the page.

Use a large-scale laminated timetable to point out the routine of the day. Have symbols for PE kit, e.g. a ball, for 'homework given out', e.g. a closed book; for 'homework in', perhaps an open jotter full of writing. Symbols can also be used for letters home and for when they are to come back. All of these and others, which the children can choose, alert those with poor planning to the days when special things have to be done. The timetable has to be big so that it does not become cluttered and confusing to the child it is meant to help.

Colour coding is very helpful and has many applications. Colour coding pegs in the cloakroom, trays, jotters, even pens, pencils and rubbers help children to identify their own things and saves squabbling. If the child chooses red as his colour, have him in the red group in class. Dots on pages to show the child where to begin and end are sometimes necessary, or if children have to do alternate sums on a page, it can be quicker to colour code them than to replan a worksheet.

Whenever possible keep a strict routine, for example always send letters home on a Friday. Then, even if the children forget, the parents know to check schoolbags and retrieve the letters before they are covered in mud off the games shoes or the juice spilt from the tumbler which has lost its lid. This avoids parents missing parents' night and wanting another appointment – so this extra preparation can pay off in the long run!

Make sure the dyspraxic children have extra tissues or wet wipes to ease visits to the toilet. And when they wish to go, don't ask them to delay. They may get little warning. Give them extra time, especially if buttons have to be undone. On the other hand they may just forget to come back – running water has a fascination for many children, so keep an eye out for them and make sure they aren't gone too long. Perhaps the classroom assistant could be earmarked to keep tabs thus ensuring the child can undertake routine jobs like taking a message to another teacher. This would give his self-esteem a huge boost. But remember, unsupervised, he may not return. As one teacher exclaimed, 'I couldn't let Ewan go with a message . . . he'd never come back!'

Teaching
Try to minimise what the children have to do without taking the responsibility away – help the children plan and organise but don't do the whole job for them. Gauge what the child can manage with support, and leave appropriate challenges.

Identify the ways the child learns best: visually, 'hands-on' or through listening to instructions. Try to present the key learning issues in ways that would be sensitive to these preferred modes. Organise the learning in short spells and give time to relax in between. Experiment having music (Mozart) playing. For some children this helps concentration, while others find this distracting, so once again be guided by the child's response.

Reduce the number of items, sums or sentences the child has to complete so that he may finish at the same time as the other children. Ask the parents or classroom assistant to scribe stories or write out sums in advance, so that the child has only to work out the answers. And as the child's planning improves, give him small responsibilities such as giving out worksheets to his own table, anything that will boost his self-esteem.

Only give essential homework as the child will be tired and will be unable to complete it well. Understand if he explains that he was too tired. Allow him to tape a story rather than have to write it.

At the start of each lesson try to provide a recap of some sort. Remember, these children can have short term memory problems and this may cause them to forget what has been taught in an earlier lesson. For the same reason dyspraxic children need extra repetition of key learning issues, which can be through word banks or through giving the children access to books to remind them of what has gone before.

Give stars for progress by all means and praise whenever praise is merited, in line with each child's ability and effort. Do not offer rewards 'for doing it more neatly' or ask the child to 'do it again'. If the work is illegible, then the child will be able to read it to you tomorrow when he is not so tired.

Use traffic lights to signal basic instructions:

- red – wait in your seat, I'm busy;
- yellow- time to tidy up or get ready;

- green – I am ready to see you now
     or Begin now!

This prevents children approaching at inappropriate times and having to be rebuffed.

Use masking tape to fix papers to the desk as this frees two hands for other jobs. Use large coloured arrows to give directions to the hall, the toilets, the library or the cloakrooms. These help children who are confused in corridors, and if the places are named, this also helps the poor readers.

Use kitchen timers so that the children have a visual picture of how much time is left. If the twisting action needed to make the timer work is difficult (two hands working together at the midline) then a large egg timer is fun and does the job just as well. The child may of course prefer to watch the sand trickling through rather than working – it could provide a distraction.

Kitchen timers can:

- indicate the amount of time left to finish a job;
- be used for 'time-out', i.e. times to relax for a moment or to regain control after a mishap (only for pupils!).

Remember that these children take things literally. 'Pull your socks up' means just that.

Above all, remember that children with dyspraxia may be impetuous and have poor self-preservation skills. I always say to my students, 'It's bad enough if the children can't read, but if they get hurt, that's far more serious.' So – if children say they can swim, check before allowing them in deep water, for they won't realise they are out of their depth. On excursions, they may dart into the road without stopping to check there is no traffic. They may hear surrounding noises, but not the cars and they are so anxious not to be last! They will get lost unless there are clear instructions, but let the children practise reading them before the actual outing.

A last word is a plea for you to remember these children have a disability. It is with them all day every day. It is not easy to have dyspraxia or for families to live with it. Children often feel they have let their families down by being like this. They are anxious not to let their school down, too. In a supportive environment they are sure to be trying just as hard as they can because they are clever children who know you are trying to help.

Getting ready for school: equipment

- Schoolbag – firmly attach a large, colourful, personal motif to help identification especially if the bag spends the day in a large box of other schoolbags. Have name and contact phone number prominently displayed inside the flap.

Choose a roomy bag with two front pockets. Always use these for the same things, e.g. pencil case in one pocket, letters home, bus passes, tissues, wet wipes (personal things) in the other. This makes packing and checking easier and quicker.

Choose Velcro fastenings or easy clips.

Inside the flap have a laminated timetable – a smaller version of the one at home and at school.

- Pencil case – a large see-through pencil case can have a list of contents fixed inside so that they can be checked. Don't have too many pens etc. If there are any special instructions, 'Go to Gran's from school today', a card in the pencil case can give a reminder and free the child from trying to retain that information all day. NB Always remember to take the card out once it has served its purpose, or the child may carry out the instructions another day. He may not be sure that he visited yesterday and go again!

- Lunch box – (packed lunches are a good idea if using a knife and fork is difficult).

  Check whether the box opens and closes easily.

  Wrap sandwich in foil, not cling film. Fillings such as cheese are easier to handle than those which make the bread soggy. Lettuce can be difficult to chew for children with poor muscle tone in the mouth. Check biscuit can be unwrapped easily – some are nearly impossible.

- Drinks – have a wide-necked stable bottle, not one that tips easily. If the child will tolerate water, this makes less mess on clothes or floors if it is spilt. Avoid cartons which need straws pushed through or tops torn off. (Two-handed coordination may be difficult and the child will squeeze the carton against the body. Then the juice spurts out and makes a mess.)

- Wet wipes – provide these to clean hands, ease toilet visits and mop spills.

- PE kit – this should be as roomy as the child will allow, to ease changing quickly. Elastic waists and Velcro fastenings make a huge difference. Provide a plastic bag for carrying dirty equipment home and if shoes are left in school, remember to check sizes as the child grows.

- School uniform – avoid laces and buttons and ties if at all possible. Have Velcro everywhere. Arrange for the teacher to have spare pants if accidents could happen. The child may wait too long before asking to go out and poor muscle control in the bladder means he is caught short. If the toilets are some way off, the child may underestimate the time needed to get there or in a panic forget where to go.

At home

Parents advise, 'Always get up early. Allow time for three things to go wrong. They always do. If the day begins in a rush, somehow the whole day goes wrong. Use lists with picture cues for the wee ones. Show the children that you are using them too, for this helps the children to realise that they are useful for grown-ups too. They also help the children become more independent. Give them special routine jobs to do, but remember they have little sense of time – allow plenty or everyone will fall out.'

- Keep the environment simple. A child who has difficulty with perceptual-motor tasks is best within a quiet, non-patterned environment. Plain carpets mean that shoes and dropped items can be easily found and plain walls mean that lists can stand out. This helps the morning speed! A large timetable is also a good idea as it reminds the child of the things he needs and what is happening that day. If it is laminated, then markings can be wiped off when routines change.
- Establish a routine. Give all the children small jobs to do such as setting the table or helping to clear away.
- Devise strategies so that the dyspraxic child can be as independent as possible:
    Decant breakfast cereal into a plastic box. This means the child can help himself.
    Don't fill jugs of juice too full or there will be spills.
    Have plastic beakers which are light but firm.
    Use sliced bread so that everyone can make their own toast.
- Make sure the chairs are at the correct height. Kitchen stools are not advised as they tip when the child leans over. They are also easily knocked over if the child is one who bumps into things.
- Have a large non-digital clock in a prominent place or set the pinger for 30 minutes before leaving.
- Make lists of routines to help the child get organised.

Example

Bedroom wall list

1. Toilet
2. Wash hands and face
3. Go down for breakfast
4. Clean teeth
5. Get dressed (a separate number chart may help the order of putting on clothes)
6. Fold pyjamas
7. Tidy room

Example

Front door list – Have you got your:

1. Schoolbag
2. Pencil case
3. Lunch box
4. Homework (Fridays)
5. PE kit (Mondays)
6. Coat and scarf?

Have a good day, love Mum.

Mums say, 'I find lists help, but we never seem to reach the last item!'

And when all of this seems just too much, we need to listen and remember what Gurney (1987) decreed. He said

Teachers and parents praise yourselves. Say out loud what you have achieved today. Tell others. For sure, they could not do as well!

CHAPTER 8

Programmes of activities

Touching and support

This is a difficult issue which needs to be discussed with school policy makers and certainly with parents. Children with dyspraxia have difficulty in feeling where their body parts are in space and so may not be able to respond to verbal instructions such as 'lift your chin' or 'hold your arms in to your sides'. And so teachers will gently adjust the position so that the child feels the correct alignment. This will probably have to happen on many occasions until the correct position is internalised. But with the current constraints on touching a child, how is this to be achieved? The answer may vary from region to region, but certainly it is critical that parents, head teachers and policy makers outside the school understand the nature of supporting the child, what it may involve and why it needs to be done. Perhaps if parents were allowed to see a demonstration of the kind of support that was envisaged, this would allay any fears. But with accusations of child abuse appearing more regularly, no teacher would want to be in a position where this could happen, so despite good relationships, it would be best to be clear about school policy and stay with it. In the past there was no problem with this kind of issue, but now, teachers and children need to be sure that all avenues of possible suspicion have been considered. The head teacher would need to be involved in any negotiation about support and probably written parental permission would need to be sought. Certainly those in authority need to be aware of the special issues which concern helping children with dyspraxia. It would be very sad if the no touching policy meant that help for the children was less effective than it could be.

Perceptual-motor programmes

The first thing to say is that many schools are convinced that their perceptual-motor programmes are helping children with dyspraxia. They speak of the children's increased confidence and competence in the hall and in tackling their daily routine. Of course it is not easy to prove that the programmes are the things that are causing the change. This could only be done if the children were in a laboratory with no extraneous influences to affect the test results. And as with any innovation, there have been some researchers who claim that such programmes are not working. Perhaps they have not been done regularly enough? Perhaps enough emphasis has not been put on the necessary standard and the activities have been rushed? Perhaps the children in some programmes were more severely disabled than in others? Perhaps too many children were taking part so that the teachers were not able to carry out the necessary observations? Perhaps the activities were not sufficiently linked to the specific difficulties the children displayed? Certainly more evaluative research needs to be done.

In the meanwhile, many teachers and parents claim that perceptual-motor programmes are the best things to offer as they can be done in school when the children are fresh; the children can be part of a group so they don't feel different in any way and the teachers who take the programmes are able to record careful observations of each child's progress. Certainly they will do no child any harm.

What should be included in a perceptual-motor programme?

Any of the activities which promote perceptual awareness and help develop the ability to move more effectively and efficiently can form part of a helpful programme. The activities should be chosen so that the children, with some effort and some practice, can be successful. A good standard of a simple movement pattern *with understanding* of how that standard was achieved is the main aim. It is important that the children recognise what they did, i.e. how their spontaneous and possibly inept efforts were altered to allow them to be successful. If this happens, there is more chance of the children being able to transfer or at least adapt these movements so that they are equally effective in different environments. A variety of activities help sustain interest and motivation and these can be chosen from:

- expressive movement activities, e.g dance and dance/drama;
- movements to promote kinesthetic awareness, poise and balance;
- planning and organisational activities, e.g. problem solving challenges;
- ball skills.

Expressive movement activities

Lots of expressive movement gives a good start to the children with poor coordination, because in dance or drama types of activity, there is no need to control equipment as is the case with ball skills and there is no large apparatus to frighten nervous children as sometimes happens in gymnastic activities. The children have only to cope with their own bodies in space and some children find this quite enough.

This is a good medium for exploring rhythm which is very helpful in learning to remember movement patterns. Furthermore the freedom within expressive movement means that a rhythm can emerge as a dance or drama sequence is composed. No external rhythm dictates as happens when music or poetry acts as a stimulus – the intrinsic rhythm comes from the type of movement chosen and develops as children work together to compose a dance phrase. Most children enjoy composing a dance based on their own selection of action words, such as 'dashing together, swirling round, then gently sinking to the floor'. As the children show the qualities of the words through their expressive movement, an intrinsic rhythmic pattern emerges and with practice, they become able to say the action words as they dance.

Expressive movement can help the development of gross motor skills when sequences include the basic movement patterns. If they are given their expressive names, then as children experience the different qualities within the movements, their vocabulary develops too.

Example: Expressive movement patterns

Walking becomes – creeping or sauntering or prowling or stalking etc.

Running becomes – dashing or darting or rushing or zipping

Jumping becomes – bounding or exploding or popping or leaping

Gesturing becomes – pointing or beckoning or turning or twisting or crumpling or stretching or sinking or growing, i.e. any action which happens 'on the spot'.

Being still becomes – freezing or holding or waiting or pausing

---

If the teacher or the children themselves select one word from each type of action, they can be ordered into an expressive movement phrase. One example could be,

---

Example: An expressive movement phrase

Dash and freeze, crumple and pop pop pop!

Analysing the expressive content of that phrase shows that contrasts in speed and distance are built in and movements on the spot give the children time to 'get ready' for the next action phrase.

Dash – moving quickly and lightly, skimming the floor for a short distance (to retain the quality of the action).

Freeze – stopping suddenly with control – in a high position because of the next action.

Crumple – sinking slowly with either a rounded or jagged action. Gathering strength – on feet ready to

Pop – exploding quickly, arms moving out from the centre of the body. Popping out to the original position ready to begin again. This might use three or four 'pops' depending on the available space.

The dance can be built into a duo with the children coming together and apart so that they develop an awareness of someone else's movement and adjust their timing and use of space to that. From duos, fours can come together to use the practised components and revamp their use of space and so compose a group dance, perhaps doing parts together or with some in sequence. Again awareness of other children, memorising the short dance and retaining the quality of the chosen movements provides an enjoyable challenge.

The children should be encouraged to select actions which allow them to show contrasts for these blend easily and very satisfyingly into a rhythmical dance. Some other examples could be, 'Swirl and hold, swirl and hold, creep away, creep away, pounce and freeze'.

In this kind of phrase, words are repeated to give time for the intrinsic rhythm to be felt. If some children find swirling difficult, they can take quite a time on the 'hold' so that their balance is re-established ready for the next phrase.

To give the dancers more travelling space, the group can be subdivided and then the children who are watching try to guess the words the dancers are demonstrating, or some try to accompany the dance with percussion, (not the music makers providing the stimulus for the dance because this would be another kind of experience where the rhythm was imposed). If this happens, then everyone is able to participate and learning words comes naturally alongside learning about the dance.

Dance drama

Once a bank of qualitative words are understood, acting out parts of stories can be fun, e.g. 'The giant stomped into the castle', or 'The tigers prowled through the long grass', for the younger ones, and 'The lightning flashed across the sky', or 'The smoke swirled from the bonfire', or 'The sea crashed onto the rocks', for the older group. The list is endless and after 'moving the words' the children should understand their meaning, where they might be applied and hopefully they will retain some to use in their storytelling or imaginative writing!

Activities for kinesthetic/body awareness, poise and balance

It is vital that the children are constantly asked to feel a good sense of poise and extension as they move and when they are still, for this promotes body and spatial awareness. It also helps breathing which in turn helps movement to be controlled.

Begin and end each session by an activity which asks the children to think about the alignment of their body and where each part is in relation to the other parts, e.g.

> Stand well. Push the back of your head high. Think about your shoulders. Are they relaxed? Shrug your shoulders and let them go – and again. Swing your arms forward and back and hold your hands into your sides. Stretch up to the ceiling and out to the side – wide as you can – wiggle your fingers and bring them in to your sides again. Is everyone steady . . . and still . . . and standing well?

> Sit down with your legs stretched out in front. Use your hands to help you balance. Can you sit tall? Are your shoulders level? Can you feel the back of your shoulders? Now spread your legs out wide and swoosh then together again – and again . . . who is still sitting tall? Look at your toes. Point them down to the floor and pull them back [the youngest ones love to say, 'Hello toes, Goodbye toes' as they do this]. 'Now cross your legs over at your ankles. Make your toes point away and pull them back up. Change your legs over . . . Are you still sitting well?

Sideways rolling on mats is good for losing and regaining a sense of balance, but teachers should emphasise the long roll – 'Can you feel your toes as you roll? – push them out?' It is also important to let the children choose their own speed. Teachers should also check that the children are able to keep their arms into their sides so that elbows are not bumped.

This detail has been set out to show that the movement is basic but is to be done well with emphasis on the children knowing where their body parts are in relation to each other, where they are in space and how moving one part affects the others.

Activities to help planning/Problem-solving activities.

While all activities help 'doing' or the execution part of moving well, the other aspects, i.e. the organising and planning of movement, have also to be considered. To achieve this it is a good idea to think of the children building sequences of movement so that they get practice in remembering what comes next. In these activities, the main thrust is to have the children tell what they plan to do and how they are going to organise themselves or their equipment, e.g. 'I'll do this and then follow with that' kind of explanation or 'I'll put the bench near the box so that I can climb up . . .'. Teachers should encourage the children to do the movements well, but initially this would be less important than the implicit planning, resourcing and remembering the movements that they have chosen to do.

Have lots of estimating games, e.g. How many long steps will you need to place the ball in the box? Which kind of ball will you choose if you are going to bounce a ball over the high skittle? (Probably a foam one would not rise high enough, the children might not have the strength to put a basketball over, an airflow one would be difficult to control, so a volleyball might be the most successful.) The children can estimate and try!

Games can include 'space' words – 'Go *under* your partner's legs. Climb *through* the barrel, go *onto* the top of the box then jump down and come back to the start.'

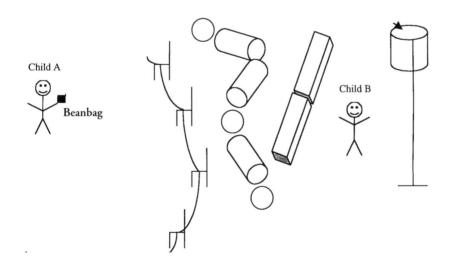

Figure 8.1 Obstacle course

Looking at Figure 8. a teacher needs to start with the aim – to get the beanbag or ball across the obstacle course and into the basket without losing it – and without touching the obstacles on the way.

The teacher then asks 'How are you going to tackle this?'

Child explains:

> 'I'll go UNDER the rope,
> THROUGH the tunnels,
> ACROSS the boxes and put the beanbag,
> UP and INTO the net.'

Adjustments can be made to add challenge for different ability levels:

- the obstacle course can be simplified or extra challenges can be added;
- another child could guard the goal to add fun but make sure that the planning is thought through first;
- the child has to keep the ball moving as he goes (bouncing the ball or dribbling a football or rolling the ball round the body);
- other children are the obstacles – perhaps sitting using their legs as scissors so that the child had to judge when to get through the barricade.

NB Even when the teacher would seem to do all the planning, e.g ' move along the bench on your back head first', there is still a lot of 'child thinking' involved in getting the movement done.

More favourite games and activities to help fine motor skills
1) Simon says 'Do this', 'Do that'

This helps copying, listening skills and body awareness. Teachers need to be sympathetic with the speed of the instructions – perhaps giving a warning 'mmmmm' before 'do that' so that the dyspraxic children have extra time to prepare.

2) Any poems or songs which have actions, e.g 'Incy Wincy Spider', 'Heads, shoulders, knees and toes', or 'In a cottage in a wood'

These games can be enjoyed by the older children if they are in a mixed age group and they feel they are showing or helping the younger ones. They are very good for finger dexterity and fitting the speed of the actions to the speed of the song.

3) Pass the parcel games

These help laterality, i.e. an awareness of 'passing to the side' and fine motor skills when the parcel has to be unwrapped. The children can sit and push the parcel round with their feet as one progression. This is difficult but fun for a brief spell.

4) Playing the piano or keyboard

This is very good for coordination and finger strengthening and dexterity.

5) Angels in the Snow

Children lie flat on floor on their backs:

(a) Sweep arms and legs wide, then together – at the same time.
(b) Sweep one arm and leg on the same side, then the opposite side, wide and together.
(c) Have children lying on their backs in a circle, fingertips touching to make an angel design. Other children, not those with dyspraxia, can run over the outstretched legs. With agile children the angels can be moving their limbs but ensure that they can follow a steady rhythm.

This is a very good way of helping children feel where the backs of all their body parts are. Old clothes help!

6) Guess the number of sweets or cubes in a jar

Unscrew the lid, tip them out and fill the jar again – minus one sweet for the guesser!

Holding the jar with one hand and unscrewing the lid is very difficult. At first the children will clamp the jar into their bodies for extra support but with practice should be able to hold it on the table to unscrew the lid.

7) Wind a lace round a bobbin

This is very difficult – a real test of fine motor skill. All sorts of threading activities can act as precursors of this one!

8) Touching, feeling

In twos children have to name parts that are being touched. The challenge is when they have to close their eyes so that feeling rather than seeing becomes the important sense.

9) Guess the letter or number

In twos, one child draws letters or figures on a partner's back. The partner has to guess what they are.

   This can be made into a game where half the class sit in a circle with their eyes closed. The other half creep in unseen and draw their own initial on the backs. The sitting child has to guess who it is.

10) All sorts of copying activities helping awareness of others, and spatial patterning

Sit facing child with two hands raised in front of each person. Draw a circle with one hand keeping the other one still. Draw a circle with the other hand. Try both hands.

Progression: draw a figure of 8

Copying is very helpful for both spatial awareness and tracking skills. Note the children's ability to track the demonstrated pattern. Gently hold their heads still if there is a lot of head turning. This encourages side vision and strengthens the muscles controlling the eyes. Try when sitting then standing.

Copying circular patterns

11) Drawing names in the air – with one hand then the other

For fun, hip mobility and control, the children can lie on their backs and draw their names with their toes!

12) Hoops

Lifting hoops over heads and climbing through – pass hoop to partner who puts feet in first then lifts it overhead – reverse.
   Build speed up into a smooth circling action.

13) Skipping rope

In twos, turning a large rope. Children with difficulties to be on one end only. Other children try to run through.

Activities to help ball skills

The main ball skills are:

- rolling
- retrieving
- throwing
- catching
- aiming.

Activities to help ball skills

1) Rolling and retrieving

Tunnels – In twos facing one another. Sitting legs outstretched and apart. Roll the ball into the gap made by the other person's legs. Then twos join up to form a circle in the same sitting position. The child with the ball chooses where to roll it and the receiver rolls the ball on into the next tunnel.

This activity helps directionality, it's fun and the speed can be varied. The good thing is that no time is lost chasing the ball to bring it back. It is firmly trapped in the different tunnels! Watch out for children having difficulty in releasing the ball and if this happens substitute a larger ball.

Rolling a ball ahead and retrieving it before it reaches a line on the floor. This involves the child running round and fielding the ball in a 'basket'.

Roll the ball against an upturned bench and retrieve it on the rebound. The actions must be quicker this time or at least they must be adjusted to suit the strength of the roll.

2) Throwing and catching

3) Throw and catch sympathetically with a partner

Aim for 10 throws without dropping the ball. Although this sounds easy, children with poor three dimensional vision will turn away rather than catch. Use a foam ball and judge how much space should be between the children. Progress to throwing 'out to the side' or lower or higher so that the throwing child must plan and the receiving child must anticipate and adjust.

Use a variety of balls as skill improves. Foam balls travel more slowly and are easily retrieved, but they don't have much 'go'. Volleyballs are best because they are the 'real thing' but are light enough not to hurt.

4) In threes, 'Donkey in the middle'

Change 'donkey' frequently and limit the area where each can go.

5) Fivers

X O X1

In threes, pass from the middle to the side and back to the middle. The middle person , O has the ball. He throws to X who throws it back. O then turns to face X1, throws the ball, receives it back and then turns to face X again. The throw is repeated to X who catches it and the two change places. This is the first sequence of five throws. X in the centre is now facing X1 and the five throws continue with the children changing places until the original positions are regained. The trio sit down to show they have completed the game. Once the routine is established the game can be a competition to see which group of three children finishes first. Having the threes lined across the hall means that all groups have the same distance to throw! This game may need to be built up slowly. It is a very good one for helping planning, for back in the classroom the children can draw out the path of the ball, numbering each throw.

6) Throwing the ball against a wall

Lots of throwing the ball against a wall and catching the rebound gives practice in judging speed, distance and direction.

7) Aiming

Skittle Alley – rolling the ball to knock down skittles helps aiming – some children can bowl the ball, others can be in charge of replacing the skittles, others can keep the score. This can be called ten pin bowling if 'alleys' are constructed. Skittles can be made with plastic bottles half-filled with sand. Younger children can make lighter skittles which will topple more easily.

Aiming high – wicker waste paper baskets tied to wallbars are marvellous for learning to aim into a basket. If these are not available, sometimes netball stands can be lowered. The action involves an overhand push and so it is important to establish the correct stance, i.e. having the opposing foot forward. Judging speed, distance and direction are all important.

Including different age groups

Most activities can suit any age group if simple alterations are made, e.g. a five-year-old could use a beanbag for throwing and catching but an 11-year-old would probably want to work with a ball. There are many sorts of balls, from foam ones which are light and don't travel too fast but don't bounce either to hedgehog balls which are hard but help children to grip. Volleyballs are much better than the heavier basketballs as they don't hurt if catches are missed and faces get bumped. So lots of variety in the apparatus gives different levels of challenge to the same task.

Similarly, difficulties can be added by changing the environment – perhaps adding more apparatus, more things to remember or perhaps having distracting movements or noises! If children have to walk along a pathway, difficulty is increased if the pathway is curved or angled or if obstacles are placed in the way so that they have to 'step over' or 'go round'. These require the children to adjust their pattern and balance demands are increased – the child will have to balance on one foot if 'stepping over' is part of the task and this can be challenging if the child tries to 'keep tall' as the adjustment is made.

Differences in speed add challenge, e.g. 'Can you throw the ball against the wall and catch it cleanly five times before I say stop?', and this can be made really tricky if someone else counts out the 1,2,3,4,5 rhythm. To experience this, ask someone to clap a regular beat and then skip down the room to it. The person clapping mustn't look and follow *your* rhythm – you must follow theirs! Other challenges can be made by altering the steepness of an inclined bench or asking children to carry out movement patterns together, e.g. 'Watch your partner as you walk along the benches and keep level'.

A final point is to remind teachers that the point of this programme is to help the children cope. Teachers are not to expect high level skill performance. A small number of basic exercises carefully chosen to help each child's profile of needs,done well and practised regularly, will suffice. Although the activities may not seem very challenging, they will stretch children with difficulties, i.e. those who can find it difficult to do things rhythmically and/or in sequence, so that an effective and efficient pattern without extraneous movements results. They have been chosen to improve the children's basic movement patterns which will hopefully give them confidence and competence throughout their day. It is a very good plan for teachers to try the movements themselves first to feel the demands made by an activity when it is done well. Good luck!

And so there are many fun ways to help children with dyspraxia. Building activities so that the balance, rhythm, timing and directionality demands gradually increase will help the children's self-awareness to develop and enable them to become more confident and competent children across the curriculum and in all the other coping skills they require at home. With a positive mentor, with practice and determination these children will soon, or perhaps a little later, be able to say, 'Look at me, I can do it too!'

A movement observation record

Child's name .... Sex ☐   ☐
                                                                   Male   Female

Age .... years .... months

This checklist is for one child who is causing you concern. Please record the child's usual level of competence rather than focusing on one unusual occurrence. If, however, the child's movement is erratic, making a general picture difficult or less than useful, please say that this is the case.

Before looking more specifically at motor development, please say whether you would consider that this was the child's only area of difficulty or whether there are other problems too.

Please tick if appropriate and add any other area of concern.

	Yes	No
Does the child have		
(a) Poor sight	☐	☐
(b) Low hearing	☐	☐
(c) A physical disability	☐	☐
(d) Difficulty in understanding instructions	☐	☐
(e) Speech difficulties	☐	☐
(f) Body-build problems	☐	☐
(i) very overweight	☐	☐
(ii) fragile	☐	☐
(iii) little strength	☐	☐
And is the child		
(g) Very tense and unsure	☐	☐
(h) Aggressive	☐	☐
(i) Lethargic – hard to interest	☐	☐
(j) Lacking persistence	☐	☐
(k) Seeking attention all the time	☐	☐

Any other difficulty? Please note below

The checklist now asks you to tick one box for each competence then give a mark out of 10 for 'general coping ability' in that field. The boxes are 'Yes, can do it'; 'Some difficulty', meaning that the child needs real effort to cope; 'Severe difficulty', meaning that the child does not cope and 'Regression' which means that the child's performance is getting worse.

NB: This is a movement observation record to help teachers compile Assessment Profiles for school use or for gaining access to specialist help. It is not a test to determine dyspraxia.

Gross motor skills

Can the child	Yes, can do it	Some difficulty	Severe difficulty	Regression	Please give details
(a) Stand still, balanced and in control?					
(b) Sit still retaining poise?					
(c) Walk smoothly and with good poise?					
(d) Turn corners efficiently?					
(e) Walk on tip-toe with control (count of 6)?					
(f) Jump (two feet off floor)?					
(g) Kick a stationary ball?					
(h) Catch a large soft ball when thrown sympathetically?					
(i) Roll sideways and recover to stand with a good sense of timing and balance?					
(j) Craw?					

Give a mark out of 10 for coordination in gross motor skills ☐

Fine motor skills

Can the child	Yes, can do it	Some difficulty	Severe difficulty	Regression	Please give details
(a) Use a pencil/paint brush with control?					
(b) Pick up and replace objects efficiently?					
(c) Use two hands together to thread beads, build Lego or do jigsaws?					
(d) Draw a person with some detail of parts?					
(e) Dress in the correct order?					

Give a mark out of 10 for dexterity in fine motor skills ☐

Intellectual skills

Can the child	Yes, can do it	Some difficulty	Severe difficulty	Regression	Please give details
(a) Talk readily to adults?					
Talk readily to children?					
(b) Articulate clearly?					
(c) Use a wide vocabulary?					
(d) Listen attentively?					
(e) Respond appropriately?					
(f) Follow a sequence of instructions?					
(g) Understand					
i. spatial concepts – over, under, through?					
ii. simple mathematical concepts – bigger, smaller?					

Give the child a mark out of 10 for intellectual competence ☐

Social skills

Can the child	Yes, can do it	Some difficulty	Severe difficulty	Regression	Please give details
(a) Take turns with no fuss?					
(b) Interact easily with other children?					
(c) Take the lead in activities?					
(d) Participate in someone else's game?					

Give the child a mark out of 10 for social behaviour   ☐

Emotional skills

Does the child

	Usually	Sometimes	Rarely	Regression	Please give details
(a) Appear confident in following the daily routine?					
(b) Constantly seek attention?					
(c) Disturb other children?					
(d) Sustain eye contact?					
(e) Cope in new situations?					
(f) Appear aggressive or defiant?					
(g) Withdraw easily					
(h) Show impulsive behaviour					

Give the child a mark out of 10 for emotional behaviour   ☐

This record could usefully be shared with other teachers, with physiotherapists, occupational therapists or psychologists i.e. with anyone who has resources to help the child.

Activities to help ball skills

The main ball skills are

rolling and retrieving, throwing and catching, aiming and kicking.

There are many kinds of balls to try. Foam ones don't hurt. Volleyballs are great because they are the 'real thing' but are light enough not to hurt.

(1) Tunnels

In twos facing one another. Sitting legs outstretched and apart. Roll the ball into the gap made by the other person's legs.

Try lots of rolling so that tracking the ball is practised, e.g rolling a tennis ball into an upturned bucket. This helps aiming skills.

Then twos join up into sixes or eights

In groups, sit in a circle in the same position. The child with the ball chooses where to roll it and the receiver rolls the ball on into the next tunnel.

This helps directionality, it's fun and the speed can be varied. The good thing is that no time is lost chasing the ball to bring it back. It is firmly held in the tunnel.

(2) Rolling a ball ahead and retrieving it before it reaches a line on the floor.

This helps judging speed, i.e estimating the pace in line with the ability to catch up.

Roll the ball against an upturned bench and retrieve it on the rebound

Again judging the speed is important. Good for varying pace.

(3) Throw underarm sympathetically to partner. Aim for 10 throws without dropping the ball.

Although this sounds easy, children with poor three dimensional vision will turn away rather than catch. Use a foam ball.
Work on the throwing arm having a smooth sweep. Say 'throw' at the moment of release if this is difficult.

(4) Catching – as above but emphasise watching the ball and having a basket ready to catch.

The alternate foot to the throwing arm should be forward to let the arm move easily. Aim for accuracy, not distance

(5) In threes, 'Donkey in the middle'
Change 'donkey' frequently.

(6) Skittle Alley (rolling and aiming)

Rolling the ball to knock down skittles helps aiming – can be related to ten pin bowling if 'alleys' are constructed.

Use a variety of balls as skill improves. Foam balls travel more slowly and are easily retrieved, but they don't have much 'go'.
This activity helps timing of releasing the ball. It gives lots of satisfaction when the skittles fall. Younger children can make skittles from plastic bottles and half-filled with dry sand and these will topple more easily than the gym ones which are hard to knock over.

(7) Throwing and aiming

Begin with a large target so that the child concentrates on the throwing action and keep the distance short to begin with. Once this is established use waste paper baskets for targets and gradually raise the height. This links with basketball and netball

This probably needs an overarm throw if the basket is even at waist height. it is important to take this slowly. Hold the ball at shoulder

(8) Kicking

Sit on a chair. Have the ball ahead of the kicking foot. Push the ball into a wide goal.

Stand with support, e.g. between two chairs. Push ball into goal. Gradually remove support and reduce size of goal.

Take two steps, begin RF. (if preferred foot) LF. and kick with RF.

Gradually use more walking steps then increase speed. Keep ball stationary. Gradually have ball moving so that the child has to judge the timing and the speed of the ball in relation to the action of the foot.

In twos kicking the ball to each other sympathetically. Use the inside of the foot to control the ball and push it to make the pass accurate.

Have a donkey in the middle game as for throwing. Build up to a two against two game.

Aim for control of the body as a kicking action can throw the body off balance if it is too fierce. Use the word 'push' rather than 'kick.' The children have to control the direction of the ball so goal posts make the activity real and great fun.

Level in the preferred hand. Support it with the other hand. Have the alternate foot forward, the body twisting to the ball side. Encourage 'pushing ' the ball till the action is steady.

Games and activities to help fine motor skills

(1) Simon says 'Do this', 'Do that'

Teacher as Simon makes different body shapes. Children copy when 'Simon says do this' but hold still on 'Do that'.

(2) Any poems or songs which have actions, e.g

Incy Wincy Spider
In a cottage in a wood

Helps finger dexterity.
Remember to give support if children are sitting on the floor.

(3) Pass the parcel games

Helps laterality – awareness of children to the side helped by passing action. Finger dexterity helped by receiving and letting the parcel go – and by pulling off the paper if this is part of the game.

(4) Playing the piano or keyboard

Marvellous for finger dexterity and control.

(5) Angels in the Snow

Children lie flat on floor

Sweep arms and legs wide, then together

Have children lying in a circle to make a star design. Older children, not those with dyspraxia, can run over the outstretched legs. With agile children the angels can be moving their limbs but ensure that they can follow a steady rhythm.

Helps body awareness of the back of the body, back of arms and legs.
Helps rhythm and needs concentration.

(6) Guess the number of sweets or cubes in a jar. Unscrew the lid, tip them out and fill the jar again – minus one sweet for the winner!

Helps finger strength and two handed coordination. Helps crossing the midline. A good activity for helping everyday coping skills at home.

(7) Wind a lace round a bobbin

This is difficult as one hand has to be still while the other is moving.

(8) In twos, children have to name parts that are being touched.

This helps body awareness and assessment of sensitivity to touch.

(9) In twos, one child draws letters or figures on the other's back. The other has to guess what they are.

This can be made into a game where half the class sit in a circle with their eyes closed. The other half creep in unseen and draw their own initial on the backs. The sitting child has to guess who it is.

Try in sitting then standing.

(10) All sorts of copying activities help awareness of others, and spatial patterning.

Sit facing child with two hands raised in front of each person. Draw a circle with one hand keeping the other one still. Draw a circle with the other hand. Try both hands.

Note the children's ability to track the pattern. Gently hold their heads still if there is a lot of head turning. This encourages side vision.

Progression. Draw a figure of 8.

Vary the size of the figure 8.

(11) Drawing names in the air – with one hand then the other. For fun and mobility lie on back and draw names with toes!

Helps mobility – not suitable for children with poor muscle tone in the shoulder girdle.

(12) Lifting hoops over heads and climbing through – pass hoop to partner who puts feet in first then lifts it overhead – reverse.

Build speed up into a smooth circling action.

Good for planning timing of actions. Do it slowly first to feel the rhythm. Watch for any unnecessary hand flapping as the child waits to receive the hoop

(13) In twos, turning a large rope. Children with difficulties to be on one end only. Other children try to run through.

APPENDIX 4

Activities to help gross motor skills

Walking
Rope or coloured tape on the floor. If there is extra hand fluttering, a beanbag in each hand can help the children feel the position of their hands.

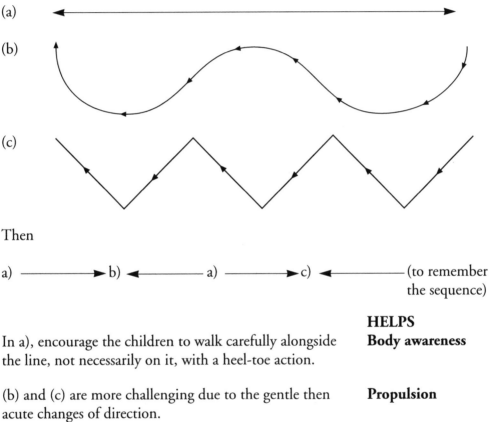

(a)

(b)

(c)

Then

a) ——————▶ b) ◀——————— a) ——————▶ c) ◀——————— (to remember the sequence)

HELPS

In a), encourage the children to walk carefully alongside the line, not necessarily on it, with a heel-toe action.

Body awareness

(b) and (c) are more challenging due to the gentle then acute changes of direction.

Propulsion

Encourage the children to move carefully and slowly, emphasising walking tall.

Good posture

Progression 1: Two children begin at different places and watch each other, aiming to finish at the same time.

Timing

Progression 2: Substitute crawling in (a). This is very important for coordination and vital if there is no climbing equipment.

Crawling

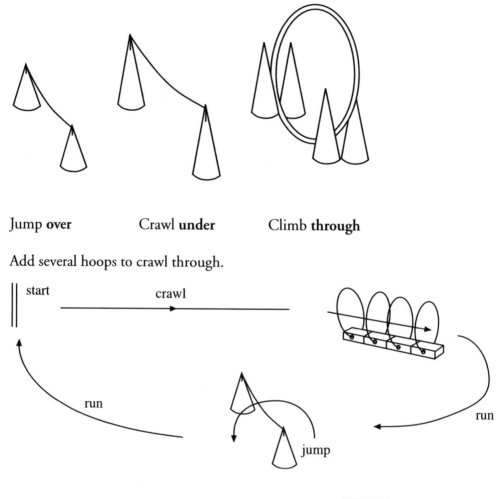

Jump **over**   Crawl **under**   Climb **through**

Add several hoops to crawl through.

Children try not to touch the hoops. Emphasise 'through', 'under' and then 'over'.	**HELPS** **Coordination,** **directionality**
Encourage children to call out directions as they move.	**Conceptual under-** **standing of spatial terms**
Progression: Children rearrange apparatus and remember spatial concepts. Older children can crawl along a box top – two sections only – remember they have to 'crawl down' back to the floor.	**Development of** **ordering**

Crawling and climbing
Crawl over a soft rolled up mat (carpet)
Crawl/climb up steps or plank (no hands as progression)
Jump down into a good space and run round to begin again

HELPS

Sequencing

Climbing actions using the recovery to aid the preparation of the next action

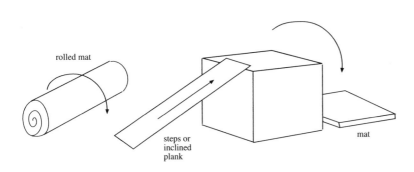

Progression:

Bunny jump over rolled carpet

HELPS Strengthening wrists (weight-bearing)

This is a good visual sequence of activities.

Emphasise standing well (pushing the back of the head up) to begin and finish.

Marching and waiting
It is important that the following activities are done calmly and carefully with no rush! Standing tall gives an important sense of poise and body awareness.

HELPS Rhythmical awareness

March forward smartly for four steps and 'wait, wait, wait'

Control

March backwards for four steps and 'wait, wait, wait'

Listening skills

Repeat adding a clap on the wait

Teacher counts out rhythmically:

1 2 3 4 and wait, wait, wait
Back 2 3 4 and wait, wait, wait
Forward 2 3 4 and clap, clap, clap
Back 2 3 4 and clap, clap, clap

Body awareness (marching tall, heads high)
Rhythm through counting to 4
Awareness of other children as they keep in line

Progression:

(a)

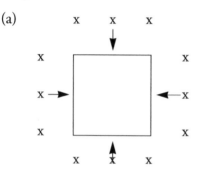

Children march to edge of carpet and back

Laterality (awareness of sidedness)

All children repeat the pattern they have already learned at the same time, perhaps substituting waving for clapping for the younger ones. Older children could clap hands with the children opposite. This would be rhythmically challenging.

(b) Children on opposite sides go in and out at different times.

Judging size of step

Allow children to march heavily if this helps some get good feedback.

Jumping
(a) Feet together

Free jumping, feet together to build consecutive actions:

Jump and jump and wait, jump and jump and wait.
Use arm swing to help propulsion forward.

Progression:

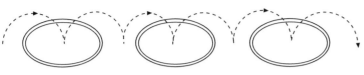

3 coloured hoops

HELPS

Coordination

Strong leg action

Continuous movement

Jump into hoops – 'Jump and jump and jump and out'; varying distance. Work for control and rhythm.

Planning and sequencing

(Some children will need to 'shuffle' to regain a good preparatory position for the next jump, while others will 'jack-in-the-box'.)

One child per large hoop

Leg strength

Control

Coordination

Rhythmic development

Jumping in and out in all directions.

Teacher can accompany with tambourine. 1 and 2 and 3 and 4 (jumps).

Rest, get ready – now you're off. 1 and 2 and 3 and 4 and stand quite still and tall.

Negotiating

Arrange bricks into paths

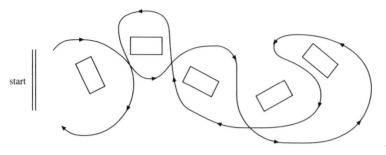

start

HELPS

Children have to stay just a whisper away but not touching, then run back. Children choose running, skipping, hopping, moving backwards.

Spatial awareness
Body boundary

Progression:

Bowl hoop or dribble football
Replace bricks with chairs
Rearrange pathway

Control and
manipulation
skills

Hopping
Hopping over line (say six hops), RF (or preferred foot)

HELPS

Balance

Coordination

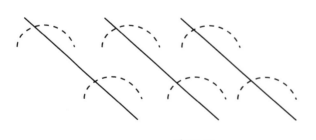

Body awareness

Partner
awareness

And again using non-preferred foot

Progression:

Two children approach at the same time, hopping four or six times
Bend down to touch other child's foot (hands on floor)
Regain standing
Change foot to hop back

Balancing

Walking along broad side of bench – head high, looking
forward

Progression 1:

Hold hoop above head as you walk. Keep hoop steady!

Progression 2:

Walking along narrow ledge of bench, with light handhold
where necessary. Then alone – trying to feel for position of
next step rather than looking down.

Progression 3:

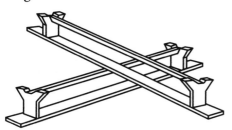

See-saw – two benches sit astride as see-saw
Teacher supervision required

Progression 4:

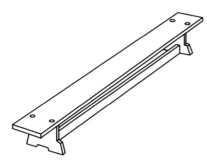

Single bench broad side up
One foot flat on broad side of bench. Push head high, come
   down to floor, push high, repeat.

HELPS

**Balance
Coordination
Timing
Partner
cooperation**

**Good poise
Body awareness
Leg
strengthening**

**Balance
Segmented
movement
Body awareness**

Keep the same foot on the bench till the end.
Repeat using other foot on bench.

Progression 5:

Use the same activity but the narrow side of the bench.   **Coordination**
Offer some light support so that the child feels the extension.
Emphasise strong straight back and legs.

Progression 6:

Using either the broad or narrow side of the bench as
appropriate – Stand well, balance on one foot, arms
outstretched.

Draw as large a circle as possible with the other foot (allow
time between turns to correct any overbalancing).
Change over so that circling foot becomes balancing foot.

Bunny jumps

(1)   Freely on floor, emphasising weight evenly balanced   **Transfer of**
         on two hands looking forward and up.   **weight from feet**
                                                                     on to strong
(2)   Over tape/rope or through hoop (trying not to touch   **arms.**
         hoop).   **Weight-bearing**
                                                                     strengthening
Progression for most agile children: **for arms/hands.**

Child A holds hoop just above floor level.
Child B bunny jumps through, Child A moving hoop to clear
feet.

Useful addresses

AFASIC (Association for all Speech Impaired Children)
347 Central Markets
Smithfield
London
EC1A 9NH   Tel No 020 7236 3632

Dyspraxia Foundation
8 West Alley
Hitchin
Hertfordshire   Tel No 01462 455016
SG5 1EG   Helpline 01462 454986

CURB
(Children under risk from bullying)
Maureen Booth-Martin
Heath
Cardiff
CF4 3NT   Helpline 02920 611300

British Dyslexia Foundation
98 London Road
Reading
Berkshire   Tel No 01189 662677

Healthcall Discovery Centre
12 Cathedral Road
Cardiff   Tel No 02920 222011
CF9 1LJ   Fax No 02920 666850

The Nuffield Centre Dyspraxia Programme
Nuffield Hearing & Speech Centre
RNTNE Division of Royal Free
Hamsptead NHS Trust
Grays Inn Road
London
WCIX 8DA   Tel No 020 7915 1535

Parents for Inclusion
Unit 20,
70 South Lambeth Road
London   Tel No 020 7735 7735
SW8 1RL   Helpline 020 7582 5008

The National Autistic Society
393 City Road
Stratford
London   Tel No 020 7833 2299
EC1V 1NG   Helpline 0870 600 8585

I – Can
4 Dyer's Building
Holborn
London
EC1N 2QP   Tel No 0870 010 4066

The Scottish Dyslexia Association
Unit 3
Stirling Business Centre
Wellgreen
Stirling
FK8 2DZ   Tel No 01786 446650

Bibliography

Aboud, F.E. and Doyle, A.B. (1995) 'The development of in group pride in black
    Canadians', *Journal of Cross Cultural Psychology* **26**.
Ainsworth, M.D.S. (1972) 'Attachment and dependency: A comparison', in J.L. Gewirtz
    (ed.) *Attachment and Dependency*. Washington DC: V.H. Winston.
American Psychiatric Association (1994) *Developmental Coordination Disorder Diagnostic
    and Statistical Manual*. Washington DC: APA.
Ayres, J.A. (1972) *Sensory Integration and Learning Disorders*. Los Angeles: Western
    Psychological Services.
Bee, H. (1995) *The Developing Child*. New York: HarperCollins College Publishers.
Bee, H. (1998) *Lifespan Development*. London: Longman Publishers.
Bee, H. (1999) *The Growing Child*, 2nd edn. London: Longman Publishers.
Blythe, P. (1992) 'A Physical Approach to Resolving Learning Difficulties'. Paper
    presented at the 4th European Conference of Neuro-developmental Delay in
    Children: Chester.
Brody, N. (1992) *Intelligence*. San Diego, CA: Academic Press.
Bruner, J. (1966) *The Process of Education*. Cambridge, MA: Harvard University Press.
Caan, W. (1998) 'Foreword', in M. Portwood *Developmental Dyspraxia, Identification and
    Intervention: A Manual for Parents and Professionals*. London: David Fulton Publishers.
Capron, C. and Duyme, M. (1989) 'Assessment of effects of socio-economic status on IQ
    in a full cross fostering study', *Nature* **340**.
Chesson R. *et al.* (1990) *The Child with Motor/Learning Difficulties*. Aberdeen: Royal
    Aberdeen Children's Hospital.
Child, D. (1986) *Psychology and the Teacher*. 4th edn. London: Holt Reinhart &
    Winston.
Cole, D.A. (1991) 'Change in self-perceived competence as a function of peer and
    teacher evaluation' *Developmental Psychology* **27**, 682–88.
Cooley, C. (1962) *Human Nature and the Social Order*. New York: Charles Scribner.
Cotrell, S. (1992) *The Effects of Obstetric Problems on Neuro-developmental Delay*. 4th

European Conference on Developmental Delay, March 1992.

Cowden, J.E. and Eason, B.L. (1991) 'Pediatric adapted physical education', *Adapted Physical Activity Quarterly* **8**, 263–79.

Dobie, S. (1996) 'Perceptual motor and neuro-developmental dimensions', in G. Reid, (ed.) *Dimensions of Dyslexia*, Vol. 2 Edinburgh: Moray House Institute.

Dunn, J. and Kendrick, C. (1982) *Sibling Love, Envy and Understanding.* Cambridge, MA: Harvard University Press.

Dyspraxia Trust (1997) *Praxis Makes Perfect.* Hitchin: Dyspraxia Trust.

Dyspraxia Foundation (1998) *Praxis Makes Perfect* II. Hitchin: Dyspraxia Foundation.

Eisenberg, N. (1992) *The Caring Child.* Cambridge, MA: Harvard University Press.

Fagot, B.I. and Pears, K.C. (1996) 'Changes in attachment during the third year: Consequences and predictions', *Development and Psychopathology* **8**.

Farnham-Diggory, S. (1992) *The Learning Disabled Child.* Cambridge, MA: Harvard University Press.

Flavell, J.H. (1985) *Cognitive Development.* New Jersey: Prentice Hall.

French, J. and Lee, M. (1996) Cited in G. Reid (ed.) Developmental Dyspraxia: an Overview, in *Dimensions of Dyslexia.* Vol. 2 Edinburgh: Moray House Institute.

Gardner, H. (1983) *Frames of Mind. The Theory of Multiple Intelligence.* New York: Basic Books.

Garmezy, N. (1993) 'Vulnerability and resilience', in D.C. Funder, R.D. Parke, C. Tomlinson-Keasey and K. Wideman (eds) *Studying Lives through Time: Personality and Development.* Washington DC: 377–98.

Gessell, A. (1925) *The Mental Growth of the Preschool Child.* New York: Macmillan.

Greenough, W.T., Black, J.E. and Wallace, C.S. (1987) 'Experience and brain development', *Child Development* **58**, 539–59.

Gurney, P. (1987) 'Self-esteem enhancement in children: A review of research findings', *Educational Research* **29**(2).

Harris, P. (1992) *Children and Emotion: The Development of Psychological Understanding.* Oxford: Blackwell.

Harter, S. (1990) 'Processes underlying adolescent self-concept formation' in R. Montemayor, G.R. Adams and T.P. Gulotta (eds). *From Childhood to Adolescence: A Transitional Period?* Newbury Park CA: Sage.

Henderson, S. and Sugden, D. (1992) *Movement Assessment Battery for Children.* New York: Harcourt Brace/The Psychological Corporation.

Kirby, A. (1999a) 'What should we call children's coordination problems? Developmental Coordination Disorder or Dyspraxia?' *Dyspraxia Review.*

Kirby, A. (1999b) *Dyspraxia: The Hidden Handicap.* London: Souvenir Press.

Lerner, R.M. (1985) 'Adolescent maturational changes and psychosocial development; A dynamic interactional perspective', *Journal of Youth and Adolescence* **14**, 355–72.

Lewis, N. (1990) 'Social knowledge and social development', *Merril-palmer Quarterly* **36**, 93–1166.

Lucas, A. *et al.* (1992) 'Breast milk and subsequent intelligence quotient in children born prematurely', *Lancet* **339**, 261–64.

Maccoby, E.E. (1990) *Social Development, Psychological Growth and the Parent – child Relationship.* New York: Harcourt Brace Janovich.

Macintyre, C. and Arrowsmith, J. (1988) *The Assessment of Motor Patterns:* Edinburgh: Dunfermline College of Physical Education.

Macintyre, C, (2000a) *Dyspraxia in the Early Years.* London: David Fulton Publishers.

Macintyre, C. (2000b) *The Art of Action Research in the Classroom.* London: David Fulton Publishers.

McClelland, D. and Kinsey, S. (1996) 'Mixed age grouping helps children develop social skills and a sense of belonging', *The Magnet Newsletter* 5(1).

Myers, B.J. (1987) 'Mother-infant bonding as a critical period' in M.H. Bornstein (ed.) *Sensitive Periods in Development: Interdisciplinary Perspectives.* Hillsdale, NJ: Erlbaum, 223–46

Pettit, G.S. *et al.* (1996) 'Stability and change in peer-rejected status: The role of child behaviour, parenting and family ecology', *Merrill-Palmer Quarterly* 42, 295–318.

Pope, M. (1988) 'Dyspraxia: A head teacher's perspective'. In *Praxis Makes Perfect.* Hitchin: The Dyspraxia Trust.

Portwood, M. (1998) *Developmental Dyspraxia, Identificaton and Intervention. A Manual for Parents and Professionals.* London: David Fulton Publishers.

Rush P. (1997) *Managing the Dyspraxic Child Through Sensory Integration Therapy.* Conference presentation: Appleford School, Shrewton.

Schaffer, E.J. (1989) 'Dimensions of mother-infant interaction: measurement stability and predictive validity', *Infant Behaviour and Development* 12.

Scottish Consultative Council on the Curriculum (1998) *Promoting Learning: Assessing Children's Progress,* 3–5.

Sternberg, R.J. (1985) *Beyond I.Q. A Triarchic Theory of Human Intelligence.* New York: Cambridge University Press.

Stunkard, A.J. and Sobel J. (1995) *Psychosocial Consequences of Obesity.* New York: Guilford Press.

Sugden, D.A. and Henderson, S.E. (1994) 'Help with movement', *Special Children* 75: *Back to Basics* 13.

Tanner, J.M. (1990) *Foetus into Man: Physical Growth from Conception to Maturity.* Cambridge, MA: Harvard University Press.

Vygotsky, L.S. (1978) *Mind and Society.* Cambridge, MA: Harvard University Press.

Wood, D. (1992) '*How Children Think and Learn.* Buckingham: Open University Press.

Index